THE COTSWOLD HOUSE

TIM JORDAN &
LIONEL WALROND

AMBERLEY

'We are apt to forget that it is in these villages the history of our country life is written, and that the sturdy yeomen who built the houses and quarried the stone and cut the timber with their own hands, formed a distinct style of architecture.'

E. Guy Dawber, 1905

First published 2014

Amberley Publishing
The Hill, Stroud,
Gloucestershire, GL5 4EP

www.amberley-books.com

Copyright © Tim Jordan and Lionel Walrond, 2014

The right of Tim Jordan and Lionel Walrond to be identified as the Authors
of this work has been asserted in accordance with the Copyrights, Designs and Patents
Act 1988.

ISBN 978-1-4456-0840-2 (hardback)
ISBN 978-1-4456-3722-8 (ebook)

British Library Cataloguing in Publication Data.
A catalogue record for this book is available from the British Library.

Typesetting and Origination by Amberley Publishing.
Printed in Great Britain.

CONTENTS

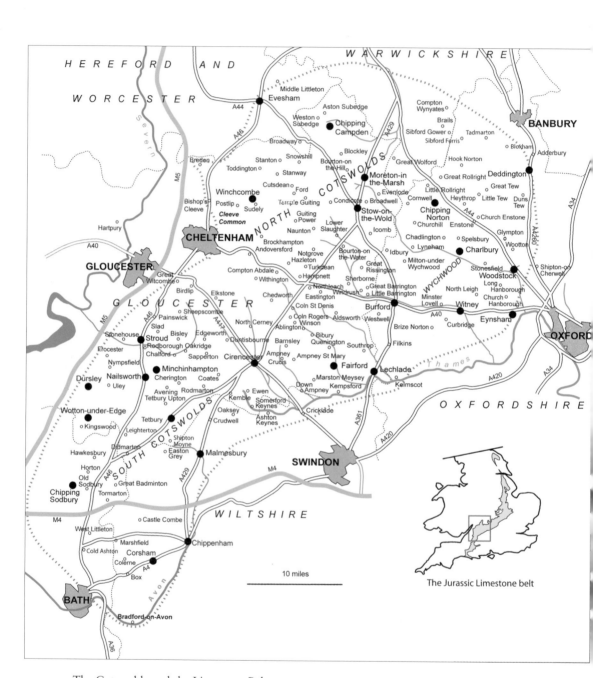

The Cotswolds and the Limestone Belt

PART I

Geography and the Story of an Evolving Style

Introducing the Cotswold House

Issues and Approaches

At the very mention of 'Cotswold Houses' what is the image that leaps to mind? What decisive factor tells you what sort of building to expect? Within the Cotswolds the house style changes from area to area, from century to century and from economy to economy. Can we define adequately what we are seeing? Clearly the immediate answer must be a qualified yes and no.

There is, as one would expect, a great variety, from humble cottages and quintessential village houses to elegant manor houses, together with a range of utilitarian as well as high-status town houses. Nevertheless, several structural elements and features give the area a number of distinctive aspects. The singular most defining characteristic must surely come from the limestone belt itself, laid down during the Jurassic period. The stone, with a succession of different layers, varies quite considerably from one locality to another. This fact alone provides the range in texture and colour, in turn reflected by the natural weathering process into the varying hues, from the greyer south Cotswold stone, through the more creamy Painswick stone to the warmer Guiting and finally the deeper ironstone in the north of the region. Its sheer workability can be seen in the numerous mullioned windows, solid chimney stacks and fine doorways and porch heads.

In the days when the transport of heavy building materials was difficult and expensive, Cotswold stone provided a ready and accessible source not just for the early great religious houses of Gloucestershire, but also after the Dissolution of the Monasteries masons continued to use the local stone in a style suited to the locality. Changing architectural styles and period influences from Tudor, Elizabethan, and Jacobean through classical, Georgian and Victorian to the Arts and Crafts Movement have all left their mark. Many of these, however, were slower in making their stylistic impact in the Cotswolds compared with other parts of the country. In the valleys of the Windrush, Leach and Coln there are numerous Tudor, Elizabethan and Jacobean houses, most having a little Renaissance detail either around the door or internally on a fireplace. Equally the

Gothic style never really died out in Gloucestershire, as David Verey has noted, surviving rather than being revived in the eighteenth century.

A major feature too is the use of stone in providing some of the most attractive roofing materials to be found anywhere. This is reflected in the steeply pitched roofs covered in an accumulation of lichen and mosses, together with their gables and dormers, often adorned with decorative finials. Here again the mason is the master, not the stone.

These manifestations often take on quite marked individual differences across the region, especially from the north to the south Cotswolds, due in no small part to differing farming, agricultural and economic factors. Ultimately of course every town and village is unique, despite and because of the oolitic limestone which gives the region so much of its character. Medieval origins are in evidence in many of the towns and villages, and a succession of enterprising manorial lords and wealthy merchants have left their marks too.

It is precisely the combination of these varying influences that explains why there are few 'pure' substantial period houses. Many may have their early origins, but they have been subjected to changes, modifications and additions over the years. Yet still they retain their underlying recognisable vernacular elements.

The book will consider each of these facets – the differing periods and styles and their characteristic features – illustrated throughout with examples from across the region as reflected in cottages, farmhouses, manor houses, almshouses, parsonages and other high-status houses, and with a concentration on the individual details which show how local craftsmen have taken a pride in their work and stamped their mark across the region. In doing so we are not attempting to break your initial image of the Cotswold house, merely to disassemble it and put it together again in order to appreciate its various parts, in order to ask ourselves how, why and when. Every little difference has a reason. The more we observe, the more we can begin to understand. The aim of this book is not to tell you what you should regard as good, but to understand the way hundreds of bits of information merge to form an entity. If we can understand why, then we are on the way to discovering an even greater pleasure in the region.

Defining the Cotswolds

Though we all seem to know what we mean when we speak of the Cotswolds, defining them has never been an easy task – not least in terms of agreeing on suitable boundaries for the region. Visually the image changes as we travel northwards, retaining a charm all the way, so that we may overlook the fact that the image may not always be exactly what we expected. We are transported not simply by its beautiful landscape but by many of them, and just as we accept the changes in the seasons, so we find ourselves accepting the Cotswolds as they are without question. Yet there is scope for just a little more knowledge in our understanding of this plot of land and the people who have helped to make it what it is.

Geographically it lies primarily in Gloucestershire, but with fringes in Worcestershire, Warwickshire, Oxfordshire and Wiltshire. We cannot, though, think of England simply in terms of horizontal bands dividing the South from the Midlands and the North. More subtle factors lie within the soil.

Geologically it is a limestone plateau with a sharper western edge, sloping gradually down to the Oxford clays in the east. In fact the limestone belt extends all the way from the Dorset coast diagonally north-east, ending up in Yorkshire. The formation of this belt is at its widest and reaches its highest levels, and arguably its most attractive and distinctive character, in the upland region we call the Cotswolds; essentially an inverted pear shape of some 60 miles or so in length and a little more than 30 miles at its widest. The rock is not uniform throughout and varies in age through millions of years and a variety of climates. It has survived earthquakes and land distortion, tropical conditions and ice ages, and in doing so has lost large parts of itself and been cut through by rivers and streams in numerous places. Clearly its most impressive and obvious border is along the north-western side where it forms an escarpment – high, steep and usually wooded. From several vantage points along this escarpment, with the river in the foreground, there is a perfect view across the Severn plain. Most of the southern and western boundaries are rounded off by beech-wooded escarpments. The wider open spaces of the northern hills contrast with the more wooded valleys and escarpment communities of the south; similarly many of the sheltered, honey-coloured villages contrast with the bleaker open expanses. Where the hills cut across the north-west corner of Oxfordshire the stone has an even deeper tint as it meets the ironstone bedrock. The stone may have changed its colour and there may be a sense of the Midlands not far away, yet there is still no obvious sign of heavy industry even though it is only some 15 miles distant. The entire eastern flank flows with no obvious topological boundary; the hills become less obvious and the streams and rivers meander eastwards, cultural features weaken, blend and then vanish almost imperceptibly. It is, however, perhaps the single element of the local limestone which unites the entire area, though we still speak of the north and south Cotswolds. This division was perhaps more apparent to local people in years gone by than it is today; we now see it as the A436 and A40 from Gloucester, skirting Oxford on its way to London.

Brief Social History Timeline

Early Norman
Each village consists of a Norman lord or his steward plus several rough-built stone huts. Occupiers all owe the lord service to work his land.

Fourteenth century
Similar, but some tenants now have timber-framed houses and pay rent – but all still owe service to the lord. Black Death brings fear and disruption to all. Much arable land put down to pasture; shortage of labour; plenty of empty houses.

Fifteenth century
Disorder of Black Death starts to have wider impact. Without proper control, house repairs use best timber, which should have been grown on for later use.

Sixteenth century
Decline of the medieval open hall. Smoke bays and later chimneys enable upper rooms to be used as parlours or for sleeping. Best timber now needed for ships with less available for houses. Stone becoming popular with all classes. Village conduct now run by manorial courts.

Seventeenth century
Rapid rise in house building and enlargements. Cotswolds now almost entirely stone, but some timber available on the Severn plain. Houses built to last.

Eighteenth century
Farmers build for long-term occupancy. Enclosure of common land. Rich get richer, poor get poorer. New class styles.

Nineteenth century
Increased population with movement into towns. Wealthy take servants, who often live in. Boys come as farm servants on yearly basis and live with the steward – resulting in low-class sleeping conditions. People now living longer, often in 'granny flat' arrangements at one end of the house.

Twentieth century
Urban and rural slums. Many interesting old houses demolished without proper record.

Setting the Scene
Landscape is an important factor in understanding why villages vary from one place to another within a region. Lush pastures and arable fields suggest a settled community. Upland areas where the soil is shallow and often stony are harder on both farmer and livestock. Equally, the accessibility of good-quality building stone is a major factor to consider.

Top: A view of the western scarp rising up from the Severn Valley towards Harescombe.
Middle and bottom: The gentler, rolling hills of the central Cotswolds.

From the Northern Uplands (*top*) to the Steeper Valleys of the South (*middle* and *bottom*)
In either case, both towns and villages are generally built just below the exposed ridges to provide at least a degree of protection from the prevailing winds.

2

HISTORICAL ELEMENTS OF AN EVOLVING
COTSWOLD STYLE

The quest to find a Cotswold style has puzzled historians for many years. The fact that no two people can entirely agree on the style itself has done little to help. There has to be a missing ingredient to the question that has compromised the picture. If we look back into local history there is a good chance we may find aspects of it.

Almost the only towns of note at the time of the Domesday Book (1086) in the Cotswolds were Winchcombe and Cirencester, with very little being known of the early villages of the region. It was not until the twelfth and thirteenth centuries that the more familiar Cotswold towns began to appear, though they obviously had existed as villages or settlements. In the northern Cotswolds, Chipping Campden is perhaps the best known of the major medieval woollen towns, and is chiefly the creation of one individual, Hugh de Gonville, who was lord of the manor in the twelfth century. He created a series of burgage plots in order to maximise the number of shop leases along the length of the High Street. Moreton-in-Marsh was built on similar principles by the Abbot of Westminster in the early thirteenth century. This relatively simple linear development is not apparent in Stow however, mainly due to its site as an important crossing point. Further south, many market towns developed along similar lines, at Minchinhampton, Tetbury, and Marshfield, resulting from landowners seeking to make their fortunes.

Medieval villages by contrast often developed in a much more scattered fashion, since space was not generally a problem in these thinly populated areas. There were more villages in the fourteenth century, but they tended to be small and more compact. Each had its church and generally there was one house larger than the rest, for the lord of the manor or his steward. Smaller hamlets often consisted only of groups of cottages around a single farmstead.

The Black Death and other plagues changed the whole nature of this society in ways that did not become fully apparent until a century or more later. Deaths in the towns may have been as high as one in three, while in the countryside, where people were more widely distributed, some places had few fatalities yet the next village could equally well have been virtually obliterated. It led to a period of great social disruption and disorientation. The manorial workforce was in turmoil; in one area alone at Ham so many died that that the lord had to hire in outside labour to gather in the harvest. Workers had to change from the skills they knew to pursue other tasks. Though very few villages were abandoned immediately in 1349, empty homes were often reoccupied despite their economic integrity having failed. The Black Death had another significant impact too from a structural point of view. Important from our perspective was the loss of the forester with his knowledge of those trees that would reach their prime for building work a century or more hence. Without his expertise and guidance the best trees were cut down prematurely, creating a potential long-term crisis. For the immediate decade or so there would have been little problem, and though the most primitive buildings simply fell down, there were ample empty properties that could be occupied and plenty of available timber to carry out immediate repairs and alterations. Only later on came the search for an alternative material. It was this chain of events which led to a period of decline, slow disintegration and the subsequent discontinuity that essentially led to the Cotswold style as we know it.

Most of the earliest surviving Cotswold houses were either manor houses, priests' houses or parts of monastic establishments. The Church was in fact a major landowner until the Dissolution of the Monasteries. The Church and various religious orders owned large tracts of land in the Cotswolds in the Middle Ages, keeping a careful eye on the wool trade – and while urging their human flocks to seek their riches in heaven, they were not averse to stockpiling substantial amounts on earth. Thus many early country houses have a monastic background and several served as summer retreats for the medieval abbots. Blockley manor, as an example, was originally the summer retreat for the bishops of Worcester.

Manors were initially a practical means of maintaining peace by way of organising petty sessions within a relatively small area which otherwise may have been quite difficult, simply due to the difficulties of travel. They were grouped into larger units called 'hundreds' (and in each the king normally held one manor as an administrative centre; others he might grant as rewards to his friends). They were also a social system, integrated with the open field system; and so the manorial system was an important influence on the later development of agriculture and the pattern of settlement. Consequently many of these early buildings should not be considered representative of the cottages of the period, of which very little is known since so few have survived.

It is important, too, in gaining some understanding of the historical development, to say something at this point about the fundamental construction process. Most early village buildings comprised only two rooms, would have been built from random rubble stone and would have required considerable repairing or rebuilding every generation or so. This was because the stone was picked up on the surface or came from quarries that were too shallow to have reached any good-quality stone. Their building stone did not have well-dressed faces and sharp corners but was rounded and did not stack easily. They had no cement, and used the local subsoil, perhaps mixed with a little lime, which would get washed out if the roof was in poor condition, which it was much of the time, being inadequately thatched. The people grew a little food for themselves and tilled the land for the lord of the manor. He also controlled large sheep walks, which came in following the Black Death, when much of the arable land became grass as there was nobody to plough. Sheep were reared not for their meat but for their wool, which was exported and was in very high demand, particularly in Italy. Beyond this, evidence is scant, except for remains where deserted villages once stood. Even in the sixteenth century a cottage would still have been tiny, built of wattle and daub or rubble, and would almost certainly have been thatched, especially in the northern Cotswolds. Stone-tiled roofs, which we see so much as being part of the Cotswolds, did not really appear until this time. Anthea Jones notes that of thirty buildings in Buckland at the end of the sixteenth century (houses, cottages and barns) only two were tiled, and two partly tiled, and there seems to be no particular social distinction about which were tiled. A similar survey in Stanway at the end of the eighteenth century showed that most of the houses were still thatched, though by now thatch was falling into less common use as many houses were either being reroofed or rebuilt. House improvement often involved inserting a floor into a one-storey building to create a bedroom upstairs. This development sometimes followed the erection of a chimney in the house where previously there had been an open hall with the fire on a hearth in the centre of the floor.

Many houses were timber framed until the fourteenth and fifteenth centuries and a substantial number still survive, particularly on the Severn plain, where they were far more common. The escarpment now forms quite a demarcation in this respect, and again the reason for much of this survival appears to lie in the soil – deeper on the plain but far less so on the stone-based higher ground. On the former, the tree roots could descend deeper into the ground for nourishment and stability with less impediment. This would be reflected in the ultimate height to which the trees would grow. That difference might not appear significant for an open-hall, single-storey house, but in the sixteenth century when upper floors began to be fashionable there was just enough headroom to insert a usable upper room on the plain. However, where shorter timbers may have been used on the higher grounds, there just was not enough headroom. There were two options: to cut off the roof, raise the wall and then reroof; or pull the entire building down and rebuild in the more fashionable stone. The first option presented considerable construction problems; new extensions to the wall posts had to be securely jointed to the old posts and now had to resist entirely different forms of stress. There seems little doubt that many houses were adapted in this way, though it is equally clear that their efforts did not for the most part withstand the test of time. Nevertheless, many of the houses in the little market towns would have been timber framed; indeed, timber framing was widespread up until the sixteenth century, when stone facades became common, as we shall note later. A substantial number of Burford's medieval buildings were timber framed, as were several in Chipping Campden and Northleach, and a number of jettied buildings still survive, though many others were subsequently stone faced. The effect of timber length is perhaps more clearly demonstrated in the Cotswolds by the fewer cruck-framed houses, though one or two examples have survived.

However, by this time our greatest forests were being drawn upon for large timbers to build and equip the Navy with larger ships to their new designs. It was soon realised that this presented a problem in our region. Large forests like Dean and Mendip were in no better shape to help. And if they could not supply, it was much less likely that the lesser woods and copses throughout the county could meet the need.

The search was on for alternative material. Brick was no doubt considered, but here too the kilns would use prodigious amounts of wood. Good building stone was available from a small number of quarries and used in churches and the grander buildings. Transportation was still a problem though, in terms of weight, distance and the state of the roads. People soon decided that quite useable stone existed on hill slopes or had been seen when digging ditches. Of the stone brought to light, most of it fell into two categories: stone that had split at an angle, producing thick chunky blocks with no smooth surfaces or useful shapes; and flattish beds a couple of inches thick and a foot or more across. The edges were irregular and somewhat decomposed by the acid solution of rainwater passing through the soil. A simple blow would, however, produce a straight edge suitable for walling.

The extensive use of this coursed rubble, usually with larger stones around the doorway and windows, is found mainly in the sixteenth century and again in the late seventeenth and eighteenth centuries. It also required the use of a somewhat stronger lime mortar. It was possible to bed the stones in natural subsoil but there was usually an admixture of slaked lime. The small surface quarries not only produced the stone for walling, but also a large amount of waste rubble, which was almost certainly fired on site, probably against an abandoned section of quarry face, to produce lime. Once fired, the resultant quicklime, together with the fine material ashes of lime, was mixed with local subsoil to form a workable mortar. Then a stronger mix was used to point the wall surface, but even this was vulnerable to the effects of weather over a period of time. To counteract this, houses and even many churches were given several coats of limewash, but with an additive. In the nineteenth century most farms would keep a half-barrel solely for this purpose, and any unused lime was left ready for the next time. Water was added, some slaked lime and then some quicklime. The latter reacted violently and the mixture became hot. Some Russian tallow or some linseed oil was then added which, because of the heat, mixed with the lime, making it waterproof. Recently some people have tried to revive the process but, noting health and safety regulations, omitted the quicklime. The mixture remained cold. The oil was not absorbed, and the entire limewash began to wash off after a few months.

Early seventeenth-century changes in iron production made quarrying easier. Stonework changed from coursed rubble to the use of massive blocks for use as quoins and sometimes in chimney construction. Then from about 1640 the shape of the quoins began to change. They were decidedly thinner and were laid on edge, rather in the manner of the 'long and short' work of the Anglo-Saxon churches.

Very different forms of settlement can be found in the steeper valleys around Stroud – almost entirely as a result of the cloth industry in the area. Here cottage construction peaked in the years between 1680 and 1740, and again between 1780 and 1830; the cottages housed large numbers of weavers who underpinned this industrial growth. Space here was more at a premium due to the steeper hillsides and the mills taking up a substantial amount of ground too. Weaving settlements, assarts, were often built on common land on the space just below the exposed hilltops. Little groups of villages were often linked by an open road, making this area quite distinct from other parts of the Cotswolds.

Another big change began to appear at the end of the same century. Classical influences had already changed the look of the stately homes, and were now working their way down the social scale. The limewashed house of a century before did not seem to give the right image. It gave way to stucco, involving a thicker base coat and a final coating of pebble-dash, which was itself set in a gruel of lime to give a gentler finish. This was an excellent medium for reserved decoration. Lintels could be outlined, quoins could receive 'egg and dart' decoration and there could be tasteful panels bearing the date and initials of the owner. But a smart exterior gives no excuse for shoddy work behind. There are instances where recent house restorations have removed the stucco to expose the stone, only to find the wall behind composed of little more than demolition debris, some of it even fire damaged.

Many, however, did not bother with the stucco at all, leaving coursed rubble exposed to the weather. Lower down the social scale there were terraces, dating probably from 1690 to 1845, where the doorways and windows used neatly cut stone, but the walls themselves were entirely of rubble lumps barely the size of one's fist, set in subsoil mortar and treated with limewash. When wet this could not have been self-supporting, so formers of wood or wattle must have been set against the inner and outer faces, the walling raised within and left for a day or so till the mud had become stable.

In fairness it must be said that between 1780 and 1825 many really good cottages of two and three storeys, sometimes as terraces, were built in the Stroud area in connection with the cloth industry. Many of these can be recognised by their cambered window and door heads. This was a relatively brief period as the cloth industry went into a fateful depression between 1824 and 1840, and hundreds of the workers were forced to leave the area, resulting in a major architectural break followed by the increasing use of locally made brick.

Finally a very different form of settlement resulted from estate villages – a product of almost total central control, owned by the nobility and gentry, many of whom had come into existence following the Dissolution of the Monasteries. Indeed, by the mid-seventeenth century, virtually the entire Cotswolds was divided into estates of varying sizes. Farms and parks demanded considerable amounts of labour and villages developed to house this workforce. Many of the landowners also had a desire to create model or picturesque developments reflecting their wealth and standing. Architectural style varied from traditional forms, through having classical overtones and occasional rustic cottages, to the Victorian Gothic at Batsford, Beverstone and Miserden. Estate villages continued to be built right up until the twentieth century, as evidenced by the Bathurst Estate centred in Cirencester, and up to and including the Arts and Crafts influence of the Barnsley brothers and Jewson, culminating in Rodmarton.

So the old vernacular traditions did not die. They were modified by such movements as the Cottage Ornée, art nouveau, Arts and Crafts and art deco, leading to major restorations by architects whose names later became world famous, many of whom came to live in the Cotswolds. The result is that whereas the vernacular traditions have almost completely died over the greater part of Britain, houses are still being built in this region that incorporate many of the original features and remain of considerable pleasure to the eye. They may be expensive, but this surely increases the appreciation of their owners, so guaranteeing their survival for the enjoyment of future generations.

Cruck-Framed Cottages

Although most buildings of the Cotswolds have stone façades, timber-framed construction was probably the norm until the sixteenth century. Cottages showing ancient cruck timbers had generally been earlier farmhouses. A few can still be found in the region.

The cruck frame seen at Didbrook (*above*) was in fact an *internal* truss, as one bay of the earlier building was removed at a later point in time, and shows a near-final phase in the rebuilding process of a house while the residents remain in occupation. They would have moved to one end as the greater part was rebuilt. The remaining old room was never rebuilt.

A cruck frame can also be seen on the end of the cottage below in Old Broadway.

Early Timber-Framed Houses
There are still a number of these visible throughout the Cotswolds, from before the more fashionable stone facing hid much of the structure of these earlier buildings.

Burford retains one or two fine examples, though the majority of its early buildings have undergone substantial changes over the years, as we will find elsewhere. Calendar's (*above*) has a fifteenth-century framed front. Winchcombe (*middle* and *bottom*) also has a number of timber-framed buildings, adding an attractive aspect to its central streets. The fact that timber framing is still in evidence is perhaps because not all of the town's inhabitants were prosperous enough to refront their properties in the now-popular Cotswold stone.

Further Examples
These buildings at Winchcombe (*above*) and Northleach (*below*) provide further evidence of the importance of these towns during this period. Northleach was a centre of considerable importance in the export of wool in the fifteenth and sixteenth centuries until much of the wool trade moved to Stroud and other areas where water supplies were better able to meet the increasing demands. Jetty construction sometimes used more timber than in box frame or cruck construction, but, as many of the timbers were shorter and used simpler joists, it was a relatively economic use of timber from the already depleted forests.

This and next page: **Aston Subedge and Weston, Didbrook and Mickelton**
Both examples show evidence of changes and additions over time. In Aston Subedge, Gardeners
Farm (*above*) was originally a sixteenth-century building with a close-studded timber frame
on one side and gable end above an ashlar-faced first floor, and an ashlar gable with later brick
additions. Brook Bend Cottage (*next page, top*) was very likely thatched initially and has an
added finer-quality ashlar porch from the rest of the building.

At Didbrook (*next page, bottom left*) and Mickelton (*next page, bottom right*), both
illustrate the low side walls of these early timber-framed cottages and the fact that the survival
of thatch is a much more common phenomenon in the northern Cotswolds.

***This and next page:* Thatch**
It cannot really be overemphasised that straw was the common roofing material on most cottages and indeed on many substantial houses, too. It was not until the seventeenth century that stone tiles began to replace thatched roofs as many houses at the time were being rebuilt. It would have started with the better homes of the merchants and leading farmers, taking centuries to work its way down to the labouring classes. One should beware, however; just because a cottage is thatched does not necessarily imply a very old building beneath. These examples are from Chipping Campden (*this page*), Stanton (*next page, top*), Broad Campden (*next page, middle*) and Combe (*next page, bottom*).

Limewashes

To protect the vulnerability of soft mortar pointing from weathering, several coats of oil-bound limewash were given, especially to rubble-stone walls. Nevertheless, this too eventually washed off, often leaving traces in the joints and on some of the stone, as we see in these examples of seventeenth-century stonework at Wotton-under-Edge (*above left*), Througham (*above right*) and Caudle Green (*below*). The latter has the unusual use of stone slates as hoods and cills to the smaller, two-light, upper-floor mullion windows.

Recent Limewashed Examples
Later use of washes was often
more for decorative or fashionable
considerations. The Dower House
at Barnsley (*top*), and Ashley Manor
and the Parsonage House at Stanton
Harcourt (*middle* and *bottom*), show
the recent use of limewashes still in
evidence.

Stucco

Earlier limewashed houses gave way to stucco, which had a thicker base coat and a final coating of pebble-dash. This allowed considerable scope for various forms of decoration, some of which can be seen on this late seventeenth-century gazebo (currently undergoing some needed renovation, *above*) at Archards on the edge of Rodborough. If stucco is later removed, the quoins may appear raised beyond the wall face, as is well shown in this window at The Hill, Stroud (*bottom right*).

Cotswold Roughcast

The Cotswold roughcast tradition remains in clear evidence on the Badminton estate, where many nineteenth-century houses retain a deep-yellow/orange limewash over the roughcast.

Neither of these last examples of stucco or roughcast are what one immediately associates with the Cotswolds, but they are nevertheless features which merit some consideration.

Stroud Area Cottages

Cottage construction in the steeper Stroud valleys peaked in the years between 1680 and 1740 and again between 1780 and 1825, largely as a result of the cloth industry, with large numbers of cottage-based weavers underpinning this growth. An early eighteenth-century example can be seen with the cross-gabled roof of Pear Tree Cottage in Nailsworth (*above left*). Here, the additional roof space would have housed a broad loom and provided further storage too. Cottages were frequently built as terraces on the hillsides and can often be recognised by their segmented window heads. The single rooms below would have been for narrow looms.

Estate Cottages

As well as providing accommodation for their increasing workforce, many of the new landowners aimed to create model or picturesque developments that reflected their wealth and standing. These had varying architectural styles. Those at Sherborne (*above*) are in quite the traditional style, albeit in groups of four. At Calmsden (*below*), the long row of cottages is more decorative, with elaborate glazing bars for the hexagonal and diamond-shaped windowpanes. Even the porches hold an interest, despite being roofed with later corrugated iron.

Badminton's Cottages

While these cottages, built in the 1860s, show some variation in form, they all have the very distinctive aspect of their orange-painted bargeboards, most with their date stones and the estate crests.

Victorian to Arts and Crafts

In Beverstone (*above*) we have an example of Vulliamy's work, where these cottages too have bargeboards, with finials above the gables, but they also have Gothic-style porches.

Finally, a group of Arts and Crafts cottages, with their distinctive diamond-shaped holes above the roof ventilators, line the road as one leaves Rodmarton (*below*).

This and next page: **Some Curiosities of the Period**

Castle Farmhouse (*this page* and *next page, top*) near Marshfield is an interesting collection of early nineteenth-century castellated buildings, an octagonal tower, a square castellated tower and a mansard roof.

Badminton has a number of curious park buildings and follies, including Slait Lodge (*next page, bottom*), with its four rounded corner towers and central chimney.

***This and next page:* Curious Lodges and an Inn**
The Ragged Cot Inn at Hyde (*this page*), built of a distinctive limestone bed quarried locally, with ashlar dressings, and Gothic windows in the gable end; all apparently providing reflections of literary romanticism.

Lodges, or gatehouses, often provide the opportunity for an exuberance in design and materials, as we see at Harescombe Grange Lodge (*next page, top*) and also Pickards Lodge, Westonbirt (*next page, bottom right*).

Farmhouses and Cottages

Where have all the farmyards gone? one might well ask. When the war broke out in 1939 they were easy to find in any village. Behind any wall you might hear the throb of activity and nearby would be the entrance to a farmyard complete with its farmhouse. Today the village is a much more silent place. The barns and various outbuildings are virtually all redundant, incompatible with twenty-first-century machinery and intensive farming. Of those that have not already disappeared many have been converted into domestic housing, especially those within the village envelope.

In the medieval period, the king owned the land, and through him the lord of the manor, who the villagers worked for. The Cotswold peasant was a copyholder; gradually these copyholds were transmuted to 'lifeholds', which were leases naming the present and future holders of the land. In a number of Cotswold villages copyholds were converted into freeholds around 1600, and lords of the manors gave up their rights to small payments from the copyholders of the area. (These were nearly all former monastic estates.) Agreements between landholders gradually whittled down the amount of common land in the Cotswolds, though at the beginning of the eighteenth century three-quarters of the parishes were still largely open. Enclosure over the next 120 years or so made large changes in the countryside (not least of all in the appearance of the many hundreds of miles of stone walls marking off the parcels of land) in attempts to use the land and manage livestock more efficiently. All of this had a considerable bearing on the house and its uses.

In addition, by the seventeenth century life expectancy was already increasing and the need for a 'granny flat' was becoming apparent. Many houses of a three-room plan made provision at one end for a granny flat on one floor or both. Here the elderly could maintain independence but always be near at hand. Later on the younger folk might rebuild their part, leaving a single-room unit to survive into the present day. Alternatively the old folk might have died and their rooms might have been used for storage, or they may have become neglected and simply tumbled down. Yet another common alternative in around 1700 was that the son built a smart new house alongside in the rising classical style; he could then use the old house as three worker's cottages, or he could install a farm manager there to run the farm.

The seventeenth century also saw the decline in the use of communal ovens, brewing and wash houses. With these various influences, room functions also began to change. Either the hall or the service area could become a kitchen. Even today, some farmers spend most of their time living in a very austere kitchen while others may retreat to somewhere cosier. Such diversity leads to major flexibility in house plans. Three rooms with a cross passage was a universal favourite, but popular changes included the reduction of the hall to a dispersal point with a staircase, and the addition of a central wing at the rear as entry into a kitchen or a dairy. A variant of this was to have some small service room in the middle, behind a passage along the front wall leading to a large kitchen at one end and a grand parlour at the other. The parlour often had a fine display of windows in the gable wall, while the front wall had a central doorway with a single-light window on either side.

Another layout quite common in Gloucestershire was the terminal hall house. The hall, now used as a large kitchen with bedrooms above, together with the cross passage, formed the main house, with the hearth on a side wall rather than in the gable. On the other side of the passage was a cross wing, hardly longer than the width of the hall, and this contained a parlour and a service room or dairy, side by side. While many houses of this layout could date from the nineteenth century, the form goes back to medieval times, and there is a fine example at Eastington on the Severn plain where the two bedchambers each have access to a double garderobe. Some smallholders in the eighteenth and nineteenth centuries built houses of a two-room plan with a lean-to roof at the back, the upper part of which, being at a lower height, could house children or servants.

Opposite page: Illustrative plans showing relationships to the medieval hall house. Gradually houses became two-storeyed with similar-sized rooms above the ground-floor rooms – the hall eventually losing its status as the principal room.

Opposite top: Simple arrangements in two-room cottages at Stanton and Snowshill.

Opposite middle: Example of a larger cottage at Aston Subedge (later the village school).

Opposite bottom: Yeoman's farmhouse at Temple Guiting showing adaptation and rebuilding of original hall.

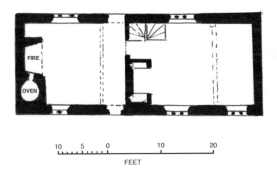

10 5 0   10   20
FEET

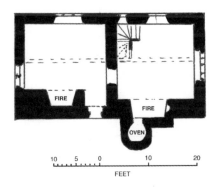

10 5 0   10   20
FEET

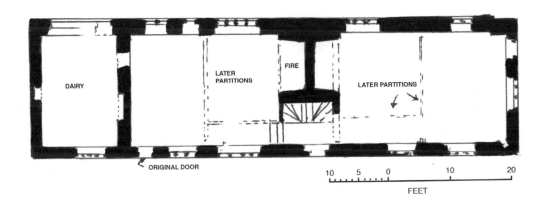

10 5 0   10   20
FEET

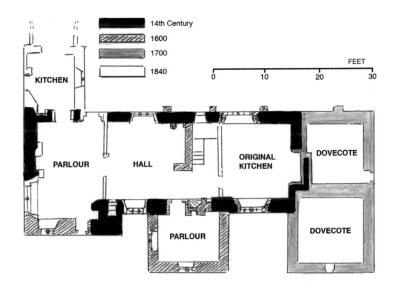

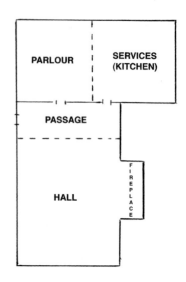

	SERVICES (KITCHEN)

PARLOUR

PASSAGE

HALL

FIREPLACE

Example of a terminal hall house. Late seventeenth century, George Street, Nailsworth (plan not to scale).

Long Houses

This is a technical term, normally relating to a rectangular building form with a living area at one end and a byre at the other, both accessed from a single entry. They were usually associated with Highland farming, and no standing examples have been noted in the Cotswolds. That said, the three-room house form has a service room below the passage which has been used for multiple purposes in addition to storing the cider barrels, cheese press and boiler that could have been used for anything from brewing to boiling pig food. A hen may be sitting on its eggs, a young calf may be tethered in one corner, and there could be sacks of chicken feed, binder canvasses, a seed drill, harvest forks and a multitude of oddments that need to be kept dry. The room might have been a later addition, perhaps on the site of an earlier cow stall. Or perhaps when the house declined from its former glory, that room was no longer needed for domestic purposes and it got used as a calf house, to protect a cow that was calving or even to house a pony. None of these made it a long house in the correct sense of the word and misuse of the term does not help us to fully understand country life.

The L-Shaped House

This form has been recognised in many regions, but never satisfactorily explained. One suggestion was that it housed an extended family, another that it was used to divide an inheritance between two brothers, or even that there were two periods of construction, with the joint between them later hidden by roughcast or a growth of ivy. A group of these houses has been noted near Stroud, not in a cluster, but widely spaced, standing each alone in separate villages or hamlets.

The intended plan seems to have comprised some five rooms, with a parlour or better room at each end and a service room where the wings join. Sometimes later changes have reversed the order, placing the parlour at the middle and the service at the end, which may make the concept more convenient for the storing of garden equipment, vegetables, etc. But it is the original purpose that concerns us. Of those that have been carefully examined, two have fourteenth-century origins, one having been enlarged in the 1590s, and the rest appear to be of the sixteenth century.

It would have been the home of the steward, and he would have been responsible to the lord for settling local land problems and the collection of rents. This would call for the holding of a court, quarterly or half-yearly. Two rooms were needed, and it is suggested that two rooms at the end of one of the wings were used for this purpose, reverting to the steward for his personal use when the duties were complete. Some of the houses still retain the word court in their house name, as at Overcourt in Bisley (see page 60).

Assart Cottages

If one examines the early nineteenth-century maps of the area between Horsley and Cranham, one notices something very odd about the distribution of the cottages on the hill slopes. Instead of following the obvious roads, they appear in small clumps, rather like frogspawn, with a narrow strip of land between each enclosed garden meandering its way up to the common land at the top. The reason is that all such cottages once stood on common land. The house was built without consent, and only then did the occupier offer to pay a fine to the lord of the manor, who did not object as the money usually went into his pocket rather than to the benefit of the community. Although one would have expected most of these cottages to be of the post-1780 cloth-boom period, some of them are from considerably earlier.

A Selection of Farmhouses, Cottages and Other Houses

We may have our own internalised perceptions of 'typical' Cotswold cottages and farmhouses, but, as we shall see, they came in quite a remarkable range of buildings, although we may still be able discern a number of common elements which have led us to this point of view. Some may be well known, others less so but still with considerable merit.

What was once a yeoman's farmhouse at Temple Guiting is undoubtedly a fine early sixteenth-century Tudor building (*above*, said to have been the summer residence of the Bishop of Oxford). The lights of the mullioned windows have four-centred heads. Like many buildings of this age, it has undergone a number of changes and additions over time (see page 39 for details). Sydenhams Farmhouse (*below*), built in typical rubble stone, has medieval origins, with two small fourteenth-century windows lighting a stone newel staircase. It too has undergone a number of changes over time, most recently an extension in the traditional style by Norman Jewson in 1930.

Laverton and Evenload

Potter's Farm in Laverton (*above*), at the foot of the scarp, is largely late sixteenth century but with later alterations and characteristic deep stone hoods over the flatter, seventeenth-century, four-centred arches above the doors.

Poplars Farmhouse at Evenlode (*below*), with coursed, squared and dressed stone, has pretty Gothic two- and three-light windows, hollow-chamfered, stone-mullioned casements with carved spandrels and leaded panes. It also has characteristic early seventeenth-century moulded cappings on its chimney stacks.

A Contrast in Styles

The farmhouse at Hawkesbury Upton (*above*) is a much simpler building, with a limewash over the rubble-stone construction of the main house but not on what was obviously an attached barn of lower status.

Top Farm, Broadway (*below*) provides another example of a more elegant seventeenth-century farmhouse.

Aston Subedge and Broadwell

The seventeenth-century Manor Farm at Aston Subedge (*above*) has had relatively little external alteration. It has three tall, gabled dormers, mullioned and transomed windows with a continuous drip mould over the ground floor and a large, gabled cross-wing.

Broadwell Hill Farmhouse (*below*), near Stow, has similar characteristics but is a much more modest, symmetrical building; however, it still has a final flourish of ball finials on its gable ends.

King's Stanley and Little Rissington

Borough Farmhouse in King's Stanley (*above*), with an elegant three-gabled frontage, has, in the top of the gables, the typical oval windows that can be seen in the Stroud area.

The farmhouse at Little Rissington (now Manor Cottages, *left*) had seven hearths in 1672. This was probably built after the copyholder became a freeholder. The house was later divided in the mid-nineteenth century. It was used by Dawber as one of his examples of Cotswold vernacular, with its attractive gabled dormers with verges, kneelers and carved finials. The chimneys have moulded caps and there are two rows of string courses along the front.

Granny Flats

Enclosure had brought about many changes in the countryside in attempts to make more efficient use of land. Furthermore, by the seventeenth century, life expectancy was increasing, often creating a need for 'granny flats'. Various changes in the use of rooms were also taking place. A case in point is shown on this original fifteenth-century building in Ebley (*above*), the cruck-framed end of which provided such accommodation when the house was rebuilt in 1681. When the turnpike was diverted from its old line, the house was rebuilt. The date stone (*inset*) was reinserted on the same side, now the back. The lower end still retains the cruck truss.

Whether this may be an explanation for the extension at a house in Little Barrington (*below*) can only be determined by internal examination.

Cottage Selection – Whittington

The following series of images provides a selection of cottages from across the Cotswolds. It will soon become apparent that there is little in the way of the 'typical' cottage. Yet, despite this, there are many elements which make up a number of recognisable features; some cottages will have several of them, others perhaps only one or two. Regardless, together they will undoubtedly go some way towards creating a general perception of a distinctive vernacular heritage – some of the details of which we will attempt to tease out in a little more depth in Part II.

Whittington is an interesting village with a number of cottages, dating from the sixteenth century to the eighteenth and beyond, all paying their rent to Whittington Court. Above is a sixteenth-century, one-and-a-half-storey row, with a substantial string course instead of separate drip moulds (and almost certainly thatched originally). A curious 1587 date stone can be seen above the doorway of No. 21 (*left*), and an even more curious 1753 sundial on another (*below*).

Little Barrington
Situated around a triangular green is a range of largely seventeenth century cottages, all different but retaining a similar scale and texture despite some being of coursed rubble stone and others of finer dressed stone with moulded architraves around the windows. Some have their stone roofs left bare at the edges, others with verges (or coping) sharpening their appearance; there is even a sash window or two, indicating later alterations.

***This spread and next page:* Bibury**
Arlington Row, Bibury's much-photographed row of weaver's cottages, was originally a
monastic wool store and barn. Because of the timber shortage, even by the 1380s each cruck
blade was made of two or three pieces pegged together instead of a single curved timber.
By the seventeenth century, the building was collapsing and internal walls and chimneys
were inserted to give support and convert it into small cottages – one of our earliest 'house

conversions'! The many dormer windows were added to make use of the top-floor space.

The cottages overleaf in Bibury show another facet of transition. The pigeonholes would indicate that these were not strictly cottages originally, as the early cottager would not be allowed to keep these birds; this was more likely the prerogative of the priest, or even a well-to-do farmer. Many of the cottages around the nearby green had wooden lintels above their windows and doors, a relatively common feature of the central Cotswolds.

Great Barrington and Hatherop

The full-height gables on the house above in Great Barrington would suggest an extended collar-beam construction and that the builder had an awareness of this in mind right from the beginning, as little external alteration appears to have taken place. The descending two-, three- and four-light windows, all with drip moulds and centrally placed, are also common features of such gables.

The cottage in Hatherop (*below*) is perhaps more characteristic of the later eighteenth century, but here we also see the addition of an extended porch to provide shelter to the door, which would normally have been exposed.

This and next page: **Upland and Northern Cottages**
Though dormers are a common feature throughout the Cotswolds, there is a greater preponderance in the north than in the south. Above we see a fine example in the upland village of Cold Aston (also still called Aston Blank) and below in Willersey, at the foot of the edge. Contrasting styles are illustrated at Bourton-on-the-Hill (*opposite top*) and Icomb (*opposite bottom*).

Porches

These change the face of the original building, but many rapidly develop as an accepted, attractive feature in their own right. These Victorian gabled porches in Winchcombe (*top*), with trelliswork, appear in perfect harmony with the gabled dormer windows above.

Others in Westwell and Lower Swell (*middle* and *bottom*) appear equally fitting.

Changing Uses; Changing Materials

The picturesque seventeenth-century cottage above in Aston Subedge has undergone a variety of changes and uses over the years, from initial domestic accommodation to schoolhouse and back to domestic use again. Holly Tree Cottage in Laverton (*below*), with its blue-slate roof, reflects the use of new materials replacing the old stone roofing tiles. These are easier and cheaper replacements, and may not be considered true vernacular, but are perfectly functional and pleasant. The characteristic hood moulds over the windows and the deep stone lintel above the doorway also mark it as a seventeenth-century building.

This and next page: **Towards the Visitor's View**
These are perhaps more towards the lasting images retained by the visitor to the Cotswolds; from the late afternoon sun across the River Eye in Lower Slaughter (*opposite top*) to the evening glow heightening the warmth of the stone cottages in Stanton (*above* and *opposite bottom*).

L-Shaped Houses

Though relatively little understood, this form has been recognised in many regions, and a number can be found in the Stroud area. Suggestions as to their purpose include the housing of an extended family, a divided inheritance between brothers and the home of the steward, responsible to the lord for collecting rents and settling local issues. Supportive of the latter, we find only one in a community, or two or three in a large parish. In Stroud itself the Rodney House is a good example (*above*), and although it has a clothier's mark and date above the porch entrance, it could well have been the site of the manorial local court.

Sydenhams (*below*) provides further illustration of this form, and has a quatrefoil ventilator.

3

SELECTED EXAMPLES OF GRANDER HOUSES
IN THE COTSWOLDS

The Cotswolds have little in the way of feudal castles, having been settled relatively peacefully since early times. Little or nothing remains of timber castles, moats and fortified manor houses beyond the occasional indicative mound, as, for example, by the manor house at Ascott-under-Wychwood.

Berkeley Castle dates from 1117, with its 1153–56 feudal shell still standing; it is undoubtedly one of the finest domestic buildings in Gloucestershire still inhabited, and is remarkable as the oldest. It is, however, just outside the Cotswold hill region proper, commanding the Severn Vale. Nevertheless, throughout its history it has had a number of important links with other significant Cotswold buildings. Nearby Beverston Castle of around 1229 is arguably the only truly Cotswold castle still standing, though its origins must actually go back even earlier. Sudeley Castle (1442) was actually a late Tudor courtier's house, later expanded into a royal palace.

Most of the earliest surviving Cotswold houses are either manor houses, priests' houses or parts of monastic establishments. Consequently these cannot be considered representative of the cottages of the period, of which little is known, as we have already observed, although by the end of the thirteenth century much of the county was included within a network of rectories or vicarages and villagers supported parish priests with their payment of tithes. Priests' houses perhaps give some of the earliest indications of better-quality buildings. At Syde there was an early, simple hall with part of its cruck roof still in place, the hall having had an upper floor inserted, probably in the sixteenth century when a fireplace and chimney replaced the smoke vent at the ridge. At the same time a stone staircase was constructed in the thick gable-end wall. The west part has a two-light, traceried medieval window.

The rectory at Buckland is one of the oldest and most complete medieval parsonages still in use as a private residence. The general consensus is that the main part was built in the second half of the fifteenth century, probably on earlier foundations. The hall has an open timber roof of two bays with a central hammer-beam truss – the ends of which are carved in the form of angels bearing shields. The cross range is later, possibly seventeenth century and, as with most houses, has undergone several subsequent modifications and improvements for modern living.

The main house of Horton Court was originally built in 1521 for William Knight, subsequently Bishop of Bath and Wells, and the court includes a free-standing north-wing Norman hall of around 1140 (the remains of a prebendal house). Both house and hall have undergone a number of changes over time. The house has a number of Renaissance features including a Tudor chimney piece with knight's arms and a Renaissance frieze. It was somewhat over-restored in 1937; the plaster ceilings date from that time and the Jacobean panelling is not *in situ*. Broad Campden provides another attractive example; a derelict Norman chapel was converted into a house, restored and extended by C. R. Ashbee in 1905–07.

The Cotswolds are overwhelmingly a region of fine market towns built on the profits of the wool trade – Burford, Tetbury, Northleach, Stow, Winchcombe, Cirencester, Painswick and Marshfield being obvious examples, with perhaps Chipping Campden being the most distinguished. The Grevel House illustrates a more urban adaptation of a merchant's house with its origins at the end of the fourteenth century. Its striking features are a two-storey bay window (indicating the position of the 'solar') and six cinquefoil-headed lights, surmounted by gargoyles. To the left is a late mullioned and transomed window; further left is a door to what was the entrance to the cross passage – indicating a transition from medieval to what was obviously considered as 'modern' at the time – all marking the emergence of a recognisable 'Cotswold' style. Opposite is the Wool Stapler's Hall, built for a leading wool merchant with a number of fine features including an oak roof with wind braces. Arlington Row, Bibury's quintessential, much-photographed row of weaver's cottages, was originally a monastic wool store and resulted from the seventeenth-century conversion of this medieval store and barn, so that all the subdividing walls, chimneys and windows are of this later date. Indeed, the crucks of the barn were in such poor condition that the insertion of the chimneys was critical in providing support for the roof. The many dormer windows were added to make use of a top-floor space.

Larger yeoman's houses would generally consist of three rooms in a row: the parlour, the hall and a service room (the hall was often provided with a cross passage). This fundamental structure has survived at Temple Guiting despite its 'modernisation' and additions during the sixteenth century (see page 39).

Many of the early country houses had a connection as summer retreats for medieval abbots (some with notable barns). The tithe barn at Stanway House was built for the Abbot of Tewkesbury. The Abbey of Tewkesbury had held the manor for 800 years and the house itself was built in Elizabethan and Stuart times by the Tracy family who acquired it in the sixteenth century. Frocester

Court and Prinknash belonged to the abbots of Gloucester and Blockley Manor is on the site of the summer residence of the bishops of Worcester. After the Dissolution it is believed that many houses were built out of the ruins of monasteries, Chavenage House being one.

Perhaps, though, the Cotswold region is best epitomised for many by its manorial architecture, and though the region had many manor houses in the medieval period, few of these were occupied by gentlemen. This was partly because the 'gentry' (a convenient term for both knights and squires in this early period) were sharply distinguished from the rest of society and partly because over a third were in ecclesiastical hands until the sixteenth century. Icomb Place, which dates from the fifteenth century, is a unique survival of a medieval knight's house. It has obviously been subjected to a number of changes over time and is currently undergoing a major renovation in an attempt to restore many of its original features. Most people, however, are familiar with the Tudor and early Stuart manor houses. These too have been adapted and modified over the years both for structural and changing style demands. Kelmscott, Daneway, Owlpen and Burford Priory are major examples with medieval origins but now must be seen as hybrids of the original buildings, much having been incorporated into later houses. Others were radically changed in the great 'rebuilding' periods of the sixteenth and seventeenth centuries. The arrival of the Arts and Crafts architects in the late nineteenth century was arguably the last big moving force behind their adaptation and repair, which has meant that there is now little in the way of any 'pure' form left.

Snowshill Manor is typical in many ways of a Cotswold manor of around 1500, with alterations in the seventeenth and eighteenth centuries. The manor house at Somerford Keynes is in a very attractive setting and is another good example of transitions through which such building have gone. The centre of the house is apparently fifteenth- or sixteenth-century with a slightly later wing on the east and a modern addition on the north-west. The older part had its roof raised to allow for another storey, so it is possible there may have been an open hall. The north entrance is also an addition.

The Tudor house (still a hall house from it medieval roots) fades virtually imperceptibly into the Jacobean house; the hall was gradually demoted from the hierarchical medieval hall to an entrance hall and private rooms. Upper Swell Manor has a fine two-storey ashlar porch with some classical grandeur. Some other notable buildings of this period are Stanton Court, Doughton Manor, Asthall Manor, Southrop Manor, Bibury Court and Chastleton House.

There was a marked building boom in the Cotswolds following the Restoration in 1660. Many of the projects owed their origins to royal connections and the new aristocracy. Politicians and court favourites were responsible for the building of Badminton, Dyrham and Cirencester House. Several of the nobility took up seasonal residence on their rural estates, often using established metropolitan architects to undertake work. Unlike their Continental counterparts, a number of English landlords often took an active interest in farming matters. One curious outcome of this was the decorative farmstead. Thomas Wright designed several castellated barns and other buildings on the Badminton Estate. The mill owners of the Stroud valleys also commissioned a number of quality projects. This was a period of compact, symmetrical houses enriched with classical detail. Nether Lypiatt Manor, for example, has been likened to a stately home in miniature.

The nineteenth century witnessed a number of different forms of revival with virtually all of the national styles represented by excellent examples across the Cotswolds. One lone and unique standout, however, is the Anglo-Arcadian at Sezincote. From the outside it is more reminiscent of a pavilion than a domestic building, though still built from a mellow-coloured stone believed to be from the Barrington area.

Opposite page: Selected Grander Houses – Castles as Domestic Housing
Castles are few in the Cotswolds due to the relatively settled nature of the region from early times. Though just outside the Cotswold region proper, Berkeley Castle (*opposite top*), dating from the twelfth century, has had a number of important links with other significant Cotswold buildings. It remains one of the oldest and finest domestic buildings in Gloucestershire still inhabited. Nearby Beverstone Castle is arguably the only truly Cotswold castle still standing, and is also in residential use. Sudeley's history goes back to the fifteenth century; it was actually a late Tudor courtier's house, later expanded into a royal palace (*opposite bottom*). It lay virtually derelict for a long period after the civil war, until sold in 1812 and again in 1830, when its current rehabilitation began.

Church Houses and Rectories

Many of the Cotswolds' surviving houses are either manor houses or are in some way linked to the Church. The fifteenth-century rubble-stone 'Priest's House' at Elkstone (*above*) was built as a church house to brew ale, so raising money for Church expenses and charity for the needy. It may well have had a timbered façade as well as its arched brace roof. A floor was inserted in the sixteenth century. The building still retains an early traceried window and a Tudor doorway, the latter now incorporated into the main house since a rear extension was added. There is also a pre-1650 mural, thought to be a composite of perhaps Ashdown House and Oxford, indicating both residential and ecclesiastical links.

The south-west part of a medieval barn at Syde (*below*) is believed to have served as a priest's house. It has recently undergone considerable restoration and changes, but a two-light, traceried medieval window is still to be seen.

Buckland Rectory and Horton Court

The fifteenth-century rectory in Buckland is one of the most complete medieval parsonages still in use as a private residence (*above*). Although it has undergone some seventeenth-century additions, the core building remains largely unaltered and the entrance is original, with an attractive oriel window. Detail of the open-hall, two-bay timber roof with a central hammer-beam truss can be seen in Part II.

Horton Court (*bottom and middle*) is largely sixteenth century but with additions and alterations in each century since. It is a prime example of the adaptations and changes that most major houses have undergone over time. It also has a twelfth-century Norman hall north wing, and in the early eighteenth century an upper floor was built across the hall for use as a Roman Catholic chapel. In 1849 this chapel was turned into a school for a time, until the hall was returned as closely as possible to its original state.

North

East

South

West

12th Century
14th Century
Early 15th Century
Late 15th Century
16th Century
17th/18th Century
19th Century

Morning Room

Dining Room

Tudor Hall
1482

Drawing Room

Norman Hall
1185

Entrance

Other Houses with Norman Elements
In Broad Campden, a long-neglected Norman chapel was restored and converted into a house by C. R. Ashbee between 1905 and 1907 and an additional wing added at the same time.

In Sherborne (*bottom*), one cottage is of particular interest as it incorporates the remains of a Norman church, including two twelfth-century doorways. The one facing the road has a carved tympanum with zigzag chevrons, but otherwise the house appears much in the traditional style.

Chipping Campden

Chipping Campden is perhaps one of the most distinguished of the Cotswold towns built on the profits of the wool trade. It certainly has a wealth of fine buildings. The late fourteenth-century Grevel House personifies a more urbane merchant's house. Its most striking feature is the two-storey Perpendicular bay window with six cinquefoil-headed lights and gargoyles above.

The Woolstapler's House (*right*), of similar date, has a stone oriel window that was restored by C. R. Ashbee in 1902.

Country Retreats

Several early country houses had connections as summer retreats for medieval abbots. The abbey of Tewkesbury had held the manor of Stanway for 800 years, and the house itself was acquired by the Tracy family in the sixteenth century (*above*). It differs from the more traditional Tudor house arrangement in that the principal rooms are in a long, south-facing range, with the hall abutting on to them at one end rather than being centrally placed. The frontage has a striking range of triple-mullioned transom windows and a large bay window below the fourth gable. It seems from internal evidence that incorporations of an earlier building were made, and the former north-east wing (on the site of the abbot's house) was demolished as recently as 1948.

Blockley Manor (*below*), on the site of the summer residence for the bishops of Worcester, is mostly seventeenth and eighteenth century, and its irregular plan indicates the number of changes and adaptations which it too has undergone over the years at the hands of its many tenants and owners. We know that, even by 1672, a Mr Hunt was paying hearth tax on seven hearths in the manor house.

This and next page: **Chavenage House**
Chavenage House, near Tetbury, is an Elizabethan manor house, and this fact illustrates the evolution of its present, E-shaped, plan and its earlier historical links with Berkeley and Sudeley. The final Edwardian wing was added in 1904.

Icomb Place

A unique survival of a medieval knight's house, the present house dates from three distinct periods; the oldest part, from the thirteenth century, includes the chapel and solar. Largely rebuilt around 1420, it has an imposing projecting gateway with a four-light Perpendicular window above and typical fifteenth-century chimney stacks corbelled over the first floor. The gateway opens into an irregular quadrangle, where further fine traceried windows have ogee arches, and leads via an early Tudor doorway to the screens end of the open hall. Following a significant period of neglect, the entire building is currently undergoing a much-needed renovation in an attempt to restore many of the original features.

Daneway House

This is another fine example of a multiphase house. The original hall house appears to date from the fourteenth century. In the sixteenth century the hall was divided horizontally, with the attic storey resting on the fine beamed ceiling of the lower room. Signs of smoke blackening in the attic can still be seen on a braced collar beam. The High Building, of five storeys and gables, was added in the seventeenth century. Other alterations were a projecting porch with room above and a 1717 sundial in the gable.

At the beginning of the twentieth century, the house was lent to Ernest Gimson and the Barnsley brothers as a showroom for their furniture and craftwork.

A Selection of Manor Houses
The sixteenth- to seventeenth-
century Westhall Hill Manor,
near Burford, forms part
of a particularly attractive
group of buildings, with some
eighteenth-century cottages
on one side and linked by a
carriage arch to a Georgian
cottage on the other, all
fronted by a small pond (*top*).
Kelmscott Manor (*centre*) is
a sixteenth-century building
with a seventeenth-century
wing added running across
the central block. Detail of the
traditional wooden guttering
chutes is illustrated in Part II.

The Warren House of 1577
in Stanton was the original
manor house; it has two
projecting gables with finials
and a wing endways to the
street. Details of the decorated
doorway to the side, with
its added enriched Jacobean
lintel, are also illustrated in
Part II.

Snowshill and Somerford Keynes

The original sixteenth-century house at Snowshill is a long, narrow and gabled building. What we see in the top image is an early seventeenth-century alteration when a projecting room was added to the west to provide a classical elevation with a hipped roof, and what is now used as the main entrance with its pedimented doorway. It is clearly not symmetrical, having three windows with transoms and mullions to the side and above the doorway and sash windows with moulded architraves and keystones on the opposite side.

Somerford Keynes Manor (*bottom*) has an early seventeenth-century core to the house, with a slightly later wing to the east and a much newer addition to the north-west. A rather curious added porch can be seen on the rear elevation, where the window mullions are both of the cavetto and ovolo type.

Upper Swell, Doughton and Bibury Court

Upper Swell Manor (*top*) is a sixteenth-century rubble-stone building, apart from the two-storey ashlar stone porch of 1625. This has a cambered pediment broken by an escutcheon of arms, Tuscan columns and the gable surmounted with ball finials.

Doughton Manor (*middle*) creates a striking image as one drives by on the way to Tetbury. It was built between 1628 and 1641, with restorations by Jewson in the 1930s. It has quoined porches and windows, with thick rubble-stone walls covered in patched lime mortar.

Bibury Court (*bottom*), close by the Coln River, is equally impressive with its multi-gabled Jacobean frontage. As the forecourt indicates, it is now a hotel.

This and next page: **North, East and to the South – Chastleton, Medford House and Dyrham**

Chastleton House (*opposite*), built in 1602 for Walter Jones, a Witney wool merchant, has been little altered over the centuries. It was sympathetically restored by the National Trust in 1997.

Medford House, Mickelton (*above*), built in 1694, is considered a textbook example of the slow transition from the vernacular Tudor Cotswold style to Queen Anne classical with its Renaissance decoration around the entrance.

What is shown here of Dyrham Park (*below*) is the early eighteenth-century addition to the original 1692 house behind. This new façade is considerably grander but still retains a domestic scale, with two storeys and an attic with large cornice above and balustraded parapet.

Nether Lypiatt Manor and Harrington House

The 1702 Nether Lypiatt Manor (*above*), near Bisley, is in many respects un-Cotswold, with its classical symmetry and pavilions either side and a splendid forecourt with ironwork gates and railings. Nevertheless, it is a very graceful building.

Harrington House (*below*), in Bourton-on-the-Water, is a fine building in regional Palladian style. Built in warm-yellow ashlar stone, it is surmounted by a domed belvedere and balustraded parapet. The interior has some elaborate rococo plasterwork, which is illustrated in Part II.

Westonbirt House and Sezincote

This nineteenth-century work by Lewis Vulliamy (*above* and page 84) is essentially an Elizabethan-style palace, the details of which are really outside the scope of summary. It is now used as a private school.

The nineteenth century also witnessed a number of other revival forms, with most of the national styles represented across the Cotswolds. Below is the unique standout in Anglo-Arcadian style of Sezincote. Faced with a very orange-coloured stone, believed to be from the Barrington area, it has the appearance more of a pavilion than a domestic building.

Next two pages: **A Composite of Town Houses** It is obviously not possible in a volume of this size to do full justice to the full range of buildings across the region. We can, as already indicated, only hope to give a flavour of its rich diversity, history and craftsmanship; and so here is a melange of town houses that we have overlooked until now. All interpretation is left to the reader at this juncture.

Broadway

Broadway

Painswick

Painswick

Broadway

Marshfield

Burford

Burford

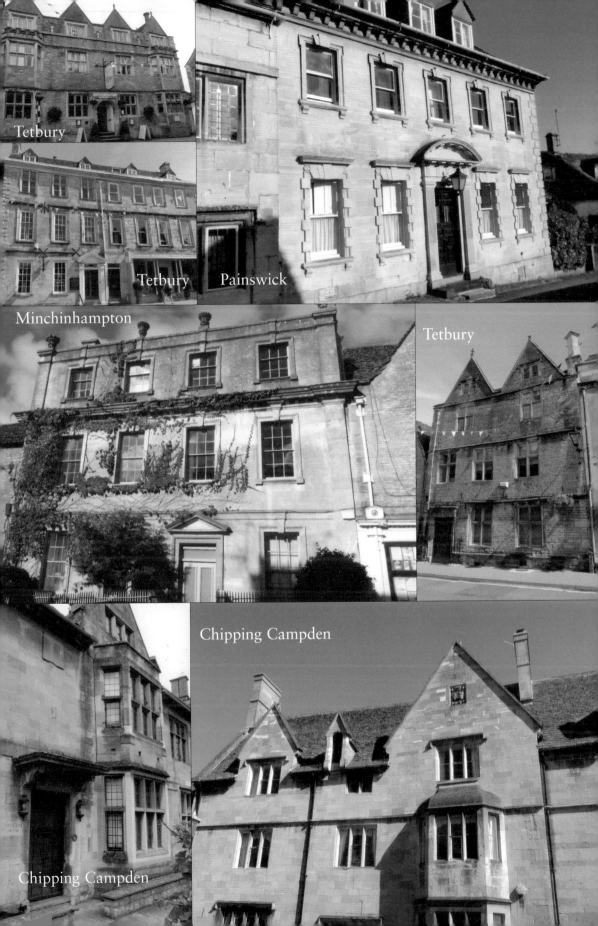

Tetbury

Tetbury

Painswick

Minchinhampton

Tetbury

Chipping Campden

Chipping Campden

4

STYLISTIC INFLUENCES AND THE COTSWOLD HOUSE NOW

Almshouses

Built as charitable residences for the poor by wealthy benefactors, who frequently used established architects, these buildings reflect virtually all of the periods we have described. Consequently, we give little description beyond their dates, and again leave the reader to appreciate their significance and contribution to the 'Cotswold style'.

Burford's 'Warwick' almshouses have fifteenth- and sixteenth-century origins and are relatively little changed outside; there are mullioned windows with metal casements and drip moulds above, and a continuous string course.

Almshouses

Chipping Campden's almshouses of 1612 (*above*) were built by Sir Baptist Hicks. Very much in the vernacular style, and regarded by Verey as the crowning achievement of seventeenth-century domestic Cotswold style and craftsmanship.

Marshfield's almshouses (*below*), founded by Elias Crispe in 1619, have a chapel and central clock tower and spire.

Almshouses

Hugh Perry's almshouses of 1638 in Wotton-under-Edge (*top*) were for six poor men and six poor women. Six gables with finials and a central domed cupola can be seen from the street.

Chipping Norton's almshouses (*middle*), a gift of Henry Cornish, gentleman, in 1640, had provision for eight poor widows. Classic Cotswold style, with a double row of continuous drip moulds creating an interesting perspective.

Spelsbury, near Chipping Norton (*bottom*), built in 1688 by John Carry, with unusual hipped roof.

Almshouses

The Witney almshouses (*top*), built in 1721 for six widows of blanket makers and rebuilt in 1868 in Gothic style, with square mullioned windows, the upper windows under pointed hoods, and tiled porches on wooden brackets.

Middle: The almshouses at Badminton, eighteenth century with three large pediments surmounted by the ducal arms.

Bottom: In Painswick, the Gyde Almshouses, built in the Arts and Crafts period, are by Sidney Barnsley and date to around 1913. This group comprises ten semi-detached, Cotswold-style cottages.

The Arts and Crafts Influences

It would be impossible to conclude this very brief overview illustrating the various transitions from local vernacular to the influences and adaptations of national styles on the Cotswolds without considering the significance of the Arts and Crafts Movement in this area. At the end of the nineteenth century the Cotswolds became both the home and inspiration of a group of writers, artists and, significantly from our perspective, architects and craftsmen who left a marked impact on the region. The relative isolation and consequent minimal effects of the Industrial Revolution on the Cotswolds ironically made it the ideal place in which to initiate a modern art movement. This was essentially set in motion by William Morris's arrival at Kelmscott. Inspired by his views, two creative settlements developed, one around Chipping Campden in the north under C. R. Ashbee, and the other in the central Cotswolds at Sapperton, Oakridge and Minchinhampton under Ernest Gimson and the Barnsley brothers.

Together they worked on the repair and adaptation of many of the outstanding medieval houses which had become neglected, as well as designing new buildings which showed the growing appreciation of a Cotswold style. They delighted in the nature of the local limestone and the individuality and craftsmanship which it had inspired, from random rubble to finely dressed ashlar, as well as the textures of the roofing materials. This was not just from an aesthetic point of view, but from the rational functionality determined by the materials themselves. They worked on Doughton, Southrop and Owlpen Manors, on Througham Court and on village halls and cottages, as well as building some of their own homes in the Cotswold style. Their importance is that they have left a legacy that is resurfacing in an awareness and growing appreciation of the importance of maintenance and conservation of traditional ideals, techniques and craftsmanship on which the Cotswolds grew.

Arts and Crafts Architectural Influences

This group of architects and craftsmen have left a permanent legacy on the region, not only in terms of their buildings but also by keeping alive an understanding of the importance of maintaining and conserving traditional techniques and craftsmanship.

At Sapperton (*above left*), Sydney Barnsley built 'Beechanger' in 1903 for himself. Just a little up the hill, Ernest Gimson built 'The Leasowes' (*below*), which was initially thatched but was altered and reroofed with traditional stone tiles after a fire.

Sapperton

Upper Dorvel House (*above* and *right*) was adapted for personal use by Ernest Barnsley from two existing cottages just below the church, also in 1903. At one end is a tall, four-storey gabled block, apparently inspired by the High Building at Daneway House.

Bachelors Court (*below, left* and *right*) was an early eighteenth-century farmhouse and cottage that was altered by Norman Jewson around 1915 and has some decorative plasterwork inside.

This and next page: **Minchinhampton and Rodborough Commons**
Silver Birches, formerly the Grey House (*this page*), was designed by Jewson. It has diamond-shaped holes above the roof ventilators, a characteristic feature of the Sapperton group. They also appear on several other buildings in the area, including a group of cottages at Rodmarton. (Were these diamond-shaped holes inspired by a similarly unique Cotswold feature on a number of earlier Cotswold barns?)

Milestone Cottage (*opposite*), designed by Thomas Falconer in 1913, also has some original door and window fittings by Alfred Bucknell.

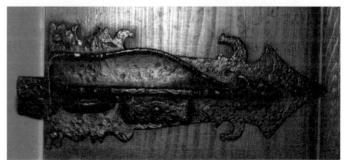

Amberley and Rodmarton

Highstones (*above*) was also by Thomas Falconer and is one of several local 'butterfly-plan' houses. These were first designed by Herman Muthesius and became quite popular in England.

Rodmarton Manor (*below*) is the largest and most important work of Ernest Barnsley, built in 1909 for the Biddulph family. The house was built entirely of local materials, including the interior panelling and fittings. The specially made furniture includes work by the Barnsleys and Gimson. It is regarded as the supreme example of a house with all its furniture made according to Arts and Crafts ideals and craftsmanship.

The Current Scene

Building has clearly continued at an increasing pace throughout the Cotswolds in recent decades, due in large part to the demands of a rapidly growing population and economic pressures. Much of it has been fairly characterless, as has been the case all over the country; but not all. Adaptations and conversions of existing buildings have continued, especially of redundant agricultural buildings in the region. Some of these have been sensitively undertaken in keeping with the local environment, some less so.

Several large housing estates on the edges of towns have made attempts to maintain a number of local characteristics, despite the density of building: some are built in stone (sometimes reconstituted, which does not weather in the same manner), some with mullion windows and other recognisable features, some with roofs of diminishing courses of tiles, albeit generally of artificial stone. One should say, though, that several of the latter products are of an increasingly good imitation, even if missing some of the essential coarser texture. It is also worth noting that a number of the old traditional stone tiles are once again being produced – admittedly at a considerable cost! At least it is hoped that this will help lessen the theft of old stone tiles from many buildings.

If planning and economic factors can be married in an acceptable manner, then not all has been lost.

Modern Houses with Elements of the Traditional Style

Several large housing estates on the edges of towns have made attempts to maintain a number of local characteristics, being built in stone (sometimes reconstituted), some with mullion windows and other recognisable features, such as roofs with diminishing courses of tiles (albeit usually of artificial stone, though 'new' traditional stone tiles are again being produced – at a cost!).

Other examples follow: the Vicarage in Church Street, Burford, was built in 1937 in the traditional style and with the traditional materials.

A twenty-first-century cottage in Whittington (*bottom*), built of local stone, has a roof dormer and gabled dormers, graduated roofing tiles and a four-centred shallow arch above the porch entrance.

***This and next page:* Other Cotswold New Builds**
A new cottage in Kingham has drip moulds above the mullions, graduated roof tiles, a dormer window set within the roof as well as a modern skylight.

   A recent new build (2000) in Sapperton is illustrated below and overleaf.

PART II

Specific Features and Characteristics

5

STONE

So, what can we deduce from this broad historical overview to enable us to recognise the Cotswold style? Clearly first and foremost are the dictates of the stone itself, both in terms of its origins and characteristics and the effects this has had on walls, roofs, windows, doorways and porches, as well as gable copings, finials and other decorative features. A number of related internal features are also worthy of consideration. Each of these will now be considered in a little more detail, essentially from a visual perspective.

Having established in our mind that the stone that underlies the Cotswolds varies slightly from place to place, that some beds can be a lot older than others, and why some contain different fossils or no fossils at all, we must think how the stone got from the ground to the walls of our houses. The immediate reply is that it came from stone quarries. True – if only it were that simple. Quarries can be very large, covering tens of acres, or so small that we barely notice them, so well has nature reclaimed its damaged land surface. But stone was also obtained using two different underground techniques.

If one wanted to build a cottage or barn, why buy stone quarried several miles away if there were beds of equal quality, though perhaps of lesser thickness, nearby on one's own land? These quarries might have been only about 4 feet deep, and when the reject material was replaced the variation in ground level was negligible. But if one's house plot was small and the stone at a slightly greater depth, then it was mined in a manner similar to that used to obtain metal ores. A shaft was sunk to find a wide joint, enabling easier removal of workable blocks. From this, a short passage was made that could be expanded into a quite large chamber. This method was very common in the south Cotswolds, especially around Eastcombe, Bussage and parts of Nailsworth, where there are still numerous such chambers waiting to be found. Each chamber produced enough stone for one building, they rarely joined up and the roofs often lie very near to the surface – to the extent that it has been known for a man to fall through into one of these chambers while deepening the floor of a cottage in Eastcombe to provide added head room. Later, when new houses were being built about a mile away, the contractors had to buy in hundreds of tons of concrete to fill old chambers before the building work could continue.

The other type of stone mine was very different. It was highly organised, and might run for many decades selling its product as far afield as London or central Wales. Some of the best examples were at Whittington and Nailsworth, where some mines have nearly a mile of galleries with a workable stone face around 30 feet high. They opened directly from a quarry face and were equipped with hand-operated winches and rail tracks leading to power-operated saws, and produced sawn paving slabs and the slightly thicker ashlar blocks for the walls of houses. These blocks were positioned to form a smooth finish, the space between each block so close as to rarely permit the insertion of a knife blade. Although ashlar-built houses commonly date from the eighteenth to the mid-nineteenth century, some of the mines could be a century older.

This and next page: **Variations in Stone Types and Colouring**
The appearance of a building reflects not only the source and quality of the stone, but also the way in which it was cut and used. Some had little in the way of mortar, though random rubble stone is a common sight throughout the region and is generally embedded in soft lime mortar. Even when coursed and roughly dressed, it requires some good-sized quoins for rigidity at the corners, allowing for a degree of settlement due to uneven ground.

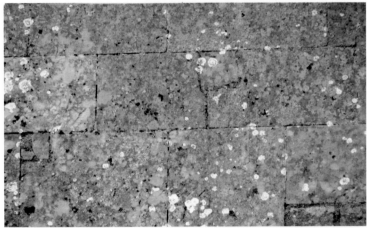

Coursed, Squared and Fine Ashlar Stone
Many fine houses, and even smaller cottages, were built of dressed ashlar blocks (albeit with rubble infilling) with fine pointing. Sometimes this would only be on the side facing the street.

Not All Was Meant to Be Seen

Basic qualities are fundamental to the use of stone in building; these include porosity, strength, colour and texture. The latter may vary considerably according to the different types even within a quarry.

Sometimes keying marks and flecks of lime show that many buildings were covered with render or limewash, especially in the eighteenth century, when taste required constructional detail to be obscured. Mortar, too, was often buttered (spread across the joints of rubble stone) to provide a smoother surface for the coats of limewash. The render was often scored to create the illusion of a better-quality squared ashlar stone.

Some stones contain the fossilised remains of ammonites, brachiopods, belemnites and other residents of the warm, shallow seas that covered the region during the Jurassic period. Some have survived almost intact, but others were crushed to dust soon after death.

This page and next spread: **Variations in Colour**

As one moves from south to north through the Cotswolds, a wide variety of stone colours in buildings have already been illustrated, from the greyer southern stone, through the creamy Painswick region (*above*), to the warmer Guiting and honey-coloured stone towards the north and the ironstone of the north-east. These all vary in hue as a result of weathering effects, and at different times of day – illustrated by the setting sun on cottages in Stanton (*next page*).

6

ROOFS

Over the centuries, the stone tiles so ubiquitous to the Cotswolds, on small and large buildings alike, have provided some of the most attractive building materials anywhere. Often referred to as Cotswolds 'slates', this is something of a misnomer as they are not slate in the geological sense. Tiles may not be a more accurate description either, since they are not manufactured but quarried from the fissile material which readily splits along bedding planes and is finally hand trimmed. There are essentially two methods of production of these 'tilestones'. The first, and indeed the oldest, is where the stone is extracted near the surface and then split. The other is where the stone is mined in large blocks, hoisted above ground and laid out to be exposed to the weather and split by frost action along its natural grain. This provides a somewhat thinner, less coarse and more regular stone tile and was produced around the Oxfordshire village of Stonesfield from the mid-sixteenth century. Either way, it was obviously not possible to supply them in consistent sizes, smaller slates being far more numerous than larger ones, and is consequently a major reason why we see them used in diminishing courses from the eaves to the ridge. Not only was it impracticable to carry the larger, heavier stone tiles up to the ridge of the roof, but before gutters became common they provided a substantial overhang at the eaves to throw the water away from the wall. Each size of slate produced had its own name and these differed in different parts of the Cotswolds. The ridge itself was generally capped with a stone crest, sawn from blocks of stone. Here are some examples of the traditional names of Cotswold slates, from the smallest to the largest:

Short Pricks	Long Bachelors	Long Fourteens
Middles Pricks	Short Nines	Long Fifteens
Long Pricks	Long Nines	Long Sixteens
Short Cuttings	Short Wibbuts	Follows
Long Cuttings	Long Wibbuts	Eaves
Movities	Short Elevens	Undereaves or Cussomes
Short Becks	Long Elevens	
Middle Becks	Short Twelves	
Long Becks	Long Twelves	
Short Bachelors	Long Thirteens	

These local characteristics undoubtedly provide an integral contribution to the vernacular architecture of the region. The irregularity of the edges, together with the graduated sizes, provide a richness of texture which many believe is unsurpassed.

Here we also see other effects of the material on design and construction, as well as that of diminishing courses – builders realised that one is dependent on the other. Such roofs are obviously very heavy and there are a number of ways of coping with this factor. One is to increase the pitch. Shallower roofs also would need larger flat slates, since smaller, uneven, coarse stones would not keep out the wet and would allow rain and snow to be easily blown under. Once the optimal

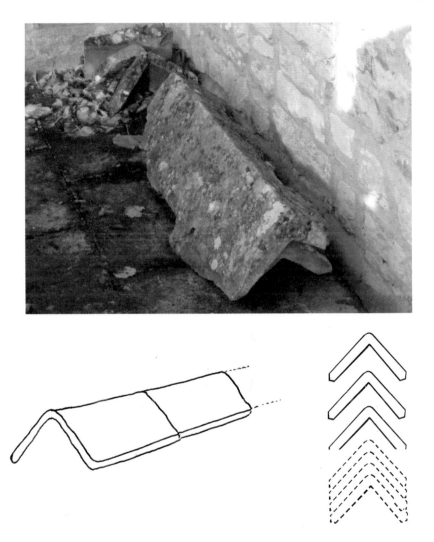

Stone ridge crests, sawn from blocks of stone.

pitch appeared to have been decided this hardly varied and we see a similar common pitch of some 55 degrees across the region. Partly due to a dearth of lead in the region, houses were generally planned so they could be roofed in one span. Hips and mitring of slates were virtually unknown; even at the junction of a lower roof with a higher one where the ridge dies in, no lead was used and it is quite common to see a length of cresting turned upside-down to throw off the water. Sometimes a series of 'steps' are seen at the side of a dormer for a similar purpose. Valleys too were formed in a wide sweep of the same smaller slates.

Cotswold slaters were clearly very skilled and could be quite inventive with the use of their slates. A further interesting example can be seen in the capping of external bread ovens and occasionally of a circular staircase.

Following the building of the Sapperton Canal Tunnel in 1789, joining the Thames and Severn, numerous mills were built in the early nineteenth century. These were largely in stone, though often with Welsh slate on the roof, as this became a common roofing material after the cutting of the Stroudwater and Thames–Severn canals.

A substantial number of Cotswold houses still retain their thatched roofs despite the significant rising cost of their maintenance. The availability of good-quality straw is obviously a factor here. Within living memory the straw from our wheat fields was relatively long. But with wartime demands on home-grown food, new strains were developed that bore a heavier yield and did not produce such long straw. The latter had the added advantage of not suffering as much from wind damage. Today, with diminished calls for straw on the farm and the use of combine harvesters, traditional binders that cut the straw without damaging it are hard to locate – strains have to be specially grown for this limited market.

Here on the Cotswolds and elsewhere we sometimes find houses with about four courses of stone slates topped up with a roof of clay tiles. A thatched roof of course does not have gutters, and it is quite possible that some of the larger stone slates were used to provide a greater overhang to protect the walls. When the thatch was later discarded, the lower courses of stone were retained and 'other' clay tiles were used thereafter.

So what else makes us so sure that stone tiles superseded thatch around 1800? Even the length of life of a stone tile is about 180 to 200 years and only a few quarries produced the best stone that would split evenly and not crumble after a few years. Some of these had been worked since medieval times, but had they been worked continuously to supply every house and barn since, they would have been exhausted long before 1800 and the scene today would have been very different. Nevertheless, a substantial amount of stone still lies close to the surface and one or two sites are again producing 'new' traditional stone tiles in places where extraction is not considered to be a blot on the landscape.

Roofs

The lower beds of the Great Oolite produce slab-like, thinly bedded stone, the raw material of traditional Cotswold roofs. A steep pitch of some 50–55 degrees is essential when rough stone slates are used, as a shallow roof would allow water to seep back and snow to be blown between. The Cotswolds certainly get sudden, squally rainstorms as well as snow, especially at the higher levels; consequently, the basic features of the vernacular make good sense in terms of the climate, terrain and material. The graduated courses and swept valleys are illustrated here, together with an upturned ridge stone protecting the junction between a dormer window ridge and the main roof slope.

Climate Protection and Effects

Above left we see the use of projecting weather stones, protecting the junction between a gable wall and lower roof on cottages in Bibury.

Weathering effects on roofs at Snowshill Manor and cottages in Great Rissington (*below* and *above right*) produce a harmony and texture which is so attractive and so characteristic of the Cotswolds.

The Slater's Skills
The skill of the slaters was also reflected in the roofing of external bread ovens where these jutted out from the main wall by a fireplace; some, however, opened on one side of the fireplace, built into the thickness of a wall. *Above left*: Rissington, *above right*: Icomb, *below*: Caudle Green.

Thatch

It is of course important to
remember that the straw thatched
roof was originally the most
common roofing material,
mainly for its cheapness and
easy availability, especially in the
north of the region, where more
corn was grown. A thatched roof
should ideally also have a steep
pitch, preferably of no less than
45 degrees. Cottages at Hidcote
and Stanton (*top, middle*) and
Great Tew (*bottom*) illustrate these
features well.

Guttering

Thatched roofs had no guttering, and neither did early stone-roofed buildings – though a number did have interesting forms of stone chutes to project the rainwater away from the walls or between the gables, as at Sydenhams Farmhouse (*above*) and at Througham and Daneway House in Sapperton (*below*).

Other Variations
Wooden chutes make a dramatic effect at Kelmscott Manor (*above*), as do the metal ones on the High Building at Daneway House (*below*).

Leadwork

The advent of lead guttering produced considerable scope for decorative effects and the recording of dates of a building or its alterations. Examples can be seen on the Old Parsonage at Buckland (*top left*), on Stokecroft House in Nailsworth (*top right*), Chastleton and Hidcote houses (*left* and *right*), right up until the climax of the Arts and Crafts Movement at Rodmarton Manor (*bottom*).

Roofs – Internal Features

So much for the contribution made by the roof to the outward aesthetic form, colour, pattern and to the landscape. To understand more we have to go inside to see what gives support to that outside image. There will be surprises, as not all roofs are the same, for reasons we shall come to understand.

Inside a medieval house of any consequence, space was dominated by the open hall extending from the ground up to the roof. One's social status was determined by what one saw in the vast timbers soaring up into the smoky gloom. Some were straight, some curved and some cut with a quatrefoil decoration. In the sixteenth century the symbols of status changed. Smoke hoods and chimneys harnessed the choking smoke and the cleaner walls now bore tapestries, murals and panelling. But let us not move too fast. There is a great deal to be learned about the structural past and its implications.

Basically, the structure of the roof space consists of two sloping timbers called principal rafters that support the roof covering. They are mortised into the ends of a tie beam which doubles as the ceiling beam of the room below. This forms a stable triangle, but the weight of the roof usually exceeds the strength of the principals. Additional timbers are needed to take the strain and we finish up with well over 100 varieties of roof construction, only a few of which will concern us.

Nearly all medieval roofs were concerned with display and what the neighbours would think. By the seventeenth century, ceilings were the fashion, and in some areas people ignored their attic space. It served no purpose other than to divert rain from soaking through to the rooms below. Elsewhere, novel ideas were resolved to convert a head-hitting, narrow, dark space into somewhere suitable for storing things, working or sleeping. The Cotswold carpenters were resourceful and came up with very effective solutions rarely seen outside the region. One of these was the extended collar truss.

A few of these trusses have been noted south of Bristol, Linda Hall found them in some sixty houses in the extreme south Cotswold area, and they abound in the Stroud valleys. Numbers decline as one moves towards the farmlands of Cirencester, but they are to be found in some of the larger houses in Wiltshire. This innovative form probably came in around the end of the fifteenth century, perhaps to give extra storage space rather than to give space for taller looms. The timber work was usually good, with carefully trimmed joists and neat joints. But there are instances of crooked, unsquared timbers and inaccurately cut joints, the entire truss looking more like a heap of fallen firewood. These may date from the late seventeenth or very early eighteenth century, when this style was becoming obsolete and good timber was unavailable, or more likely the work of a young amateur making a first, and only, attempt.

The line of the eaves was raised by some 12 to 18 inches above the ceiling beam and a large dormer constructed on one or both side walls, coinciding with the position of one of the roof trusses. Instead of the short collar beam a longer, stouter timber was used, supported at its end by the dormer. Instead of the principal supporting the collar beam, the collar now supported the principal, the lower part of which was no longer needed. A stouter timber was also needed to support the roof in the gulley between the roof surfaces, and this usually rested on a small corbel of wood or stone visible inside the attic. This form of roof gave additional space both sideways and upwards, enough to operate a broad loom within the space. It was also possible to place short boards on the upper purlins on all four sides, on which to store additional wool, bobbins, etc.

Cruck trusses have been noted in considerable numbers throughout the highland areas, west of an imaginary line through Devon, the Severn basin, and up through to the north-east of England. Regionally they vary in detail, and one specific form has been noted in the Severn plain, the distribution of which extends as far north as Shrewsbury. Having examined a number of cruck buildings in 1982 and noting they represented a number of regional forms, Prof. Maurice Barley (having first suggested all the forms had emanated from Shrewsbury) later agreed that it was more likely that the forms were attracted towards that town by its mercantile shipping trade. On the higher ground of the Cotswolds very few have been noted, just enough to suggest they may once have been rather more common. Basically, the two beams forming a cruck were produced by splitting a curved tree trunk, sitting their ends on a low sill wall, and joining their upper ends to support a ridge beam. There were a number of variant forms, as seen in the great barns of Frocester, Stanway and Bradford-on-Avon.

Another variant was the upper cruck, where the cruck sat on a tie beam near the top of a wall, creating a tall, wide attic space. There is reason to think that some of these (for example a cottage formerly at the top of Stroud High Street) must have been genuine medieval crucks, although there is a large group of roof trusses that might technically be called upper crucks but must be ruled out by virtue of their late date, around 1780 to 1825. These, then, are best termed knee-ended principal trusses (cf. Brunskill, fig. 203, p. 150, and see page 124).

These have been seen in mills and houses, but seem to have been most common in terraced cottage blocks of two and three storeys, stone built with wooden windows, and were common in the upper parts of the Stroud valleys. By their use the attic space is changed from a claustrophobic triangular space into an airy open room, well lit by windows in the roof. The principal rafters appear perfectly normal, slightly thinner than a century before and probably sawn. Where they meet the wall they turn sharply into a deep groove in the walling, concealed altogether if the wall happens to have been plastered, and are mortised into the ceiling beam of the room below. Since the likelihood is that such cottages were built to house cloth workers, these attics way well have been built to contain hand looms. In one such group of five cottages at Leonard Stanley, the ceiling–floor rafts through the entire block were not only pegged together but were secured by very long iron bolts running the entire length as well as the width. Not surprisingly, their demolition presented problems.

Another late roof form seen from time to time had an 'interrupted tie-beam truss'. As in the roof type described above, the stone wall rose considerably above the ceiling beam. An upright was secured into the principal and the ceiling beam below, and into it a short length of tie beam ran from the post back to support the end of the principal. This had the effect of dividing each side wall into a series of bays. This house type seemed to be of a much more domestic nature, and though they were there for structural reasons they could have served to divide the allotted space between the beds of live-in servants.

Roof Trusses

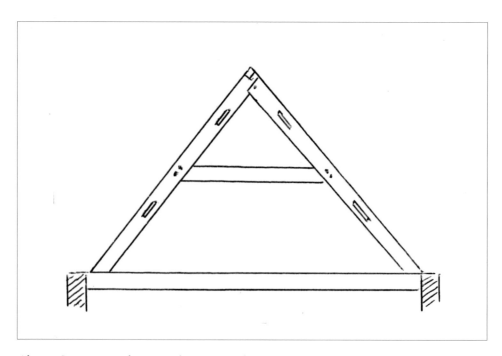

Above: Common roof truss, early seventeenth century.

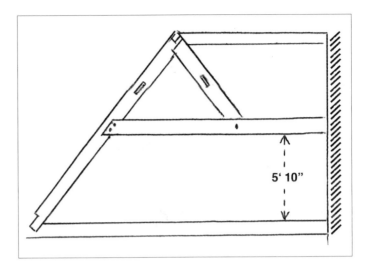

5' 10"

Extended collar truss (to scale), The Boot Inn, Horsley (demolished).

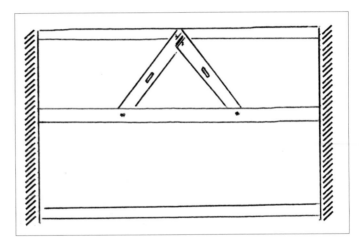

Extended collar truss, gable on both sides, increasing the floor area.

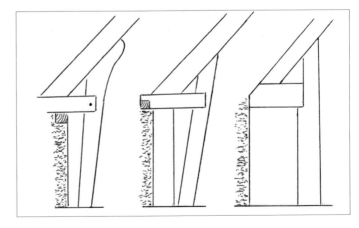

Variations of the interrupted tie-beam truss. *Left and centre:* details from Damsell's Mill, Painswick. *Right:* Elm Tree Cottage, Standish (demolished).

The Medieval Open Hall Roof

Social status in medieval houses of any consequence was frequently determined by what one saw: vast timbers rising up into the smoky gloom, dramatic wind braces and, in some cases, elaborate decoration. Buckland Rectory (*above* and *below left*), thought to be perhaps the oldest and most complete rectory in the county, has such an impressive timbered hall, dating from the fifteenth century and with angels bearing shields carved on the two central hammer beams of the roof.

Icomb Place was rebuilt in 1420 and a large proportion of the building survives, including the great hall, with its braced collar beams and two tiers of wind braces (*below right*).

Elements of Internal Roof Structures

The fifteenth-century 'Priest's House' at Elkstone (*top* and *middle*), built as a church house with first-floor hall and open roof of arched brace type, illustrates the essential roofing structure before ceilings became the fashion.

In the roof space at Salmon Springs (*bottom*) we see a good example of the extended collar providing additional space for the weaver's loom.

Structures Only Seen on Demolition

Much later, at Leonard Stanley during demolition, we see the extreme height of the end timber below the knee and the position of the wall plate. This type of roof created a much larger working area within the roof space (the structure only becoming apparent on demolition).

7

WINDOWS AND DOORWAYS

The location of the windows is an important element in the Cotswold style. As already noted, due to the structural needs of rubble walling, windows are usually positioned as far from the corners as possible. After the mid-seventeenth century they were generally placed on the centre line of a gable end.

These stone-mullioned windows, often with their lead-latticed panes and wrought-iron casements, frequently had a label or drip moulding above. Sometimes this would be carried round the building as a string course.

The earliest mullions were hollow or concave, often accompanying the Tudor or Gothic shaped head. These were followed by ovolo-moulded mullions and later by plain chamfered mullions, the latter becoming universal throughout the region for many years, even when other aspects of a house had been changed or altered.

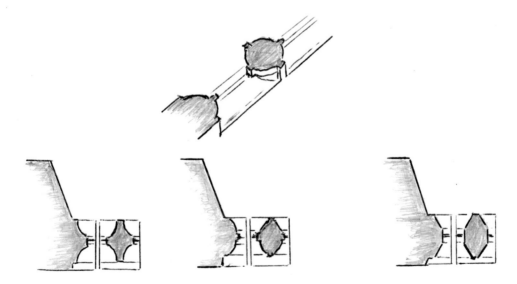

Types of Cotswold mullion mouldings, with approximate dates when commonly used. *Left:* cavetto (concave), 1550–1630 and 1675–1690. *Centre:* ovolo (convex), 1620–1660 and 1670–1720. *Right:* chamfered (stepped or plain), 1600–1750, continuous in all periods.

In early wooden windows, not those of casement or sash form, the diamond-set mullions rarely had glass or other material to keep the weather out. It is surprising how much light got past mullions of this form, and yet they were effective in keeping out rain and wind. There was also a sliding shutter on the inside. Mullions that are more widely spaced with an iron stanchion between them suggest the window was glazed with small, diamond-shaped glass panes, set in lead with lead straps to tie them to the iron stanchion. If one was truly wealthy in medieval times and had to go away for a couple of weeks, the glazing would be unfastened and packed for reaffixing in the rooms in which they would be staying.

Nevertheless, the windows retained their traditional form, with sizes being remarkably similar – the mullions some 5 to 5¼ inches wide and the central, larger, ones 8 to 10 inches. Typically the space between mullions was some 12 to 16 inches and some 2 to 3 feet in height. It would seem that virtually every village mason understood and kept to these proportions.

The number of lights, in most instances, diminish with each succeeding storey – with the ground floor generally having four or sometimes six lights with a heavier central king mullion, the next storey three and the gable two. Invariably the practice was to lessen the number of lights in the gable ends as the windows ascend. Until the second half of the seventeenth century there was a very strange reluctance to put large windows in a gable wall. Admittedly that was the usual place for the chimney, but even if the hearth was moved to a side wall there was for a time a very clear reluctance to take advantage of this space. This may very well be due to the ill-founded belief that the entire weight of the roof was hung from the ridge, which therefore needed all the support it could get.

The symmetrical disposition and squareness of the plans, together with the roofing being under one span, meant the windows could be easily arranged to come centrally under the gable in each case.

In many houses dating from the late sixteenth and early seventeenth centuries we see an arched shaping of the window heads – an echo of the Perpendicular work of the preceding century which lingered for quite some time in a number of villages until gradually the square lintels became universal. Relieving arches are not often seen at this time, but were quite common in the south Cotswolds.

A good example of these shaped heads can be seen in the attractive early sixteenth-century yeoman's farmhouse at Temple Guiting, at one time the summer residence of the Bishop of Oxford.

There was a more widespread use of window glass by the seventeenth century compared with the medieval period, when it was a luxury. Much of this was made in Bristol, Woodchester and Gloucester, using locally obtained sand, bracken and charcoal. This glass had a greenish tint with minute surface ripples, yet was surprisingly thin. The less wealthy used cloth, vellum, horn or even waxed paper, and the really poor were still using waxed paper till well into the nineteenth century. As the price of glass fell, the lights became wider, using square instead of diamond-shaped panes.

Keeping the cold air out was always a problem, though people were more used to it than we are today. The worst time was from 1597 to 1697, when temperatures dramatically fell and remained low for a century. We seem not to take into account this factor when looking at the architectural changes that took place during that century. Later on, large shutters were fixed to the outside walls, and inside there were shutters that folded away against the thickness of the wall. Sometimes the metal catches and hinges survive from the outside shutters, retained for a different reason: if they opened out directly onto a road, it could have been as protection from passing cattle perhaps on their way to market. We also know that many houses and even shops boarded their windows on fair days as a protection against drunken revellers.

With this gradual change in style towards the end of the seventeenth century, and the introduction of classical detail, the lights became wider and higher, and as rooms became loftier, transoms and upper lights were inserted, stabilising the central mullion. This formed a feature of the Queen Anne classical style which was so different from that of the traditional vernacular.

Bay windows, though not common in smaller houses, were occasionally used to good effect in towns and village streets, and sometimes the bay was brought out square from the front.

Sometimes an oriel window was used, corbelled out from the main wall – but these can hardly be classed with genuine Cotswold work and are distinctly of an earlier date. An interesting and rather curious example of what appears to be an Arts and Crafts wooden bay window can be seen in Nailsworth.

If the attic space was to be sealed off, or at least not in daily use, it was common to insulate the floor by filling the space between the joists with a mixture of waste lime plaster nodules and wheat dust, the debris from wheat ears after threshing. Oat dust and that of the best wheat would have been fed to the cattle, but wheat dust that was stained or damaged was devoid of nourishment and had little or no food value, so was used as insulation. It still contained the dust of broken wheat grains and weed seeds invaluable to 'evil spirits' for food and bedding. Children and servants sleeping in the rooms below this insulation would often hear noises above them in the dead of night and attribute them to evil spirits and be forbidden from going into the loft. But those houses with an unglazed top window had far less trouble from these spirits, protected perhaps by the frequent appearance of an owl. We now know these spirits were in fact the cavortings of rats and mice, a prime food for the owl. That topmost window in the gable, usually of but a single light and often oval or circular, came to be known as an owl window. But purists will tell you the name came from 'oillet', a small eye, and owl holes are a more specific feature of barns, where the intention was to keep down the rodent population. Say what you will, both adherents stick to their own views.

Windows

The stone mullion windows of the Cotswold region are undoubtedly a major characteristic feature. It is generally on the grander houses that early medieval windows survive, though there are some fine examples on other buildings too.

A surviving fourteenth-century window can be seen at Skinner's Mill, Painswick (*above*), and small medieval lancet windows at Sydenhams are illustrated below left, lighting an internal circular staircase. On the right is some splendid Perpendicular tracery at Icomb Place, near Stow-on-the-Wold.

Hood Moulds

A substantial variety of late medieval windows can be seen in these examples from Burford, with their metal casements and cross-leading panes of glass. These also illustrate an answer to the problem of having window openings in walls that have no guttering above, which meant that much of the rainwater would simply run down the face of the wall and over the window. A solution was the development of the hood or drip mould, a projection of dressed stone above the window and with a label at either end, allowing the water to drip clear and prevent it from blowing back.

Security and Elizabethan Grandeur

By the mid-sixteenth century, when the period of great rebuilding was starting, the first 'standard' windows began to appear, often with ecclesiastical-looking arched heads to each window section or light, as at the Warren House in Stanton (*above*). Since security was still an issue, these had strong *ferramenta* fixed in the openings, with the leaded glass usually fixed outside – though here it is on the inside.

Chavenage House (*below*) provides a magnificent two-storey window lighting the main hall.

Positioning of Windows

Not only were windows generally placed as far away from the corners as possible due to the structural demands created by rubble walling, but by the mid seventeenth century they were usually placed on the centre line of gable ends, with a diminishing number of lights from the ground floor upwards to the dormers, normally of two lights, as at Broadway (*above left*). Ground-floor windows of four to six lights often had a more pronounced central, or king, mullion for additional strength illustrated at Stanton (*above right*) and Burford (*below right*).

Window lights had generally lost their arched tops by now, too. Drip mouldings may also run above the windows in a group, as at Rissington (*below left*), and especially on the more symmetrically built cottages like this one at Burford.

Relieving Arches and Small Side Lights

Stone relieving arches began to be seen at this time too, particularly between 1580 and 1640, and these were generally more common in the south Cotswolds. These arches helped to take the weight off the mullions, especially as they became thinner. Examples are seen at Tetbury (*above left*) and Bibury (*below*).

Single lights on either one or both sides of a central doorway often indicated a form of cross passage, with large rooms at either side and service rooms between. It is likely that this example at Western Subedge (*above right*) illustrates such a transition. The insertion of a ceiling into the open hall led to a revision of the uses of all rooms. The ground-floor chamber became a parlour, and food was prepared in a kitchen rather than in the hall. One resolution was to have a large room at either end, the parlour and the kitchen/dining room, and between them a through passage and a much-reduced hall.

Timber Mullions

Ovolo-moulded mullions were also occasionally built in timber, as were these early seventeenth-century ones at Burford (*above*). The left-hand one has a scalloped edge with ball decoration, whereas the one at 96 High Street is of a simpler design, with a wooden lintel, as is the one in Stroud (*below*).

Cross-Mullions or Transoms

As windows became larger, lighting higher-ceilinged rooms, horizontal mullions (transoms) were added to provide additional support. Medford House in Mickelton (*top*, around 1694) not only shows these, but also provides a good example of the transition from the vernacular Cotswold to Queen Anne style, with classical elements and its emphasis on symmetry and some Renaissance decoration around the doorway.

The centre photograph is a further example at Fifield, and Stanford House in Chipping Campden (*bottom*) has an unusual arrangement of individual transom windows. To the right of the door and above are paired ones, and to the left are four-light windows – possibly indicating a later alteration, with the paired lights having been moved together to reduce the window tax!

Sash Windows

Fifty years later sash windows were the fashion, and many houses had them added at this time. Barton House (*above*), near Temple Guiting, an early eighteenth-century house, shows this transition, with its mullioned transom windows on the sides and sash ones in the middle and over the pedimented doorway.

By the mid-eighteenth century, many older buildings were given new sash windows and some in the towns had the smart stone surrounds, often with a keystone above, that the fashionable townspeople aspired to. The Catherine Wheel Inn, Marshfield, together with its modillion cornice and balustraded parapet, shows these well, especially the early thick glazing bars and small panes. Horizontal sliding (Yorkshire sash) windows were the poor man's version – fitted into an existing window opening and not requiring pulleys and boxing, as at The Olive Tree in Nailsworth.

As Windowpanes Got Larger…

New technologies enabled larger panes of glass to be made and this is reflected in the upper windows getting wider, as at Lion Cottage, Nailsworth (*above left*), and the six-over-six sash windows with narrower window bars at Stoke Croft (*above right*). The latter has the usual Nailsworth oval windows in each of the gables. A further fine example is illustrated by the farmhouse at Caudle Green (*below*).

Metal Casements and Furniture
Casement windows (with a hinged, opening section) can provide a wide variety of associated furniture in the form of hinges, catches, stays and handles. A small selection from Longborough (*above*), Guiting Power (*right*), Stroud (*below left*) and Broad Campden (*below right*) are illustrated here.

Decorative Fasteners

The decorative fasteners above are from Blockley Manor (*left*) and Chavenage House (*right*).

Several houses and cottages in the Stroud area have the unique type of window furniture below, which combines the functions of the catch, stay and handle. Attached near the top of the casement is a long iron bar with a number of holes at intervals along its length, the shank of which is twisted.

This and next two pages: Oriel and Bay Windows

Oriel windows project forward from the wall face, usually carried on stone brackets, as here at Rissington (*above*) and Witney (*next page*).

Bay windows, unlike oriels, extend to the full height of each storey and can take a variety of forms, such as the canted and bow types found at Burford (*right*), Bourton-on-the Hill (*page 141, top*) and Blockley (*page 141, bottom*). Often they were used as shops before village shops were purpose built.

Nineteenth-Century Variations

Not what one immediately thinks of when considering Cotswold vernacular, but many Cotswold terraces have cambered windows, and during the early nineteenth-century weaving boom many cottages, like these at Paganhill near Stroud (*above*), were built to provide workshops for the growing number of employees.

Left is a rather unusual Arts and Crafts bay window in Nailsworth.

Dormer Windows

No description of windows can be complete without considering dormer windows, one of the most characteristic features of Cotswold houses and cottages. As with many Cotswold vernacular features these were introduced for very functional reasons: to let more light into the low-ceilinged attic floors than could come from windows in the gable ends alone.

The dormer window was essentially a clever device to light the dark area under the roof, and so provide sufficient light for it to be used as a room. Thus in many small, single-storey houses the walls continue upwards by anything from a few inches to a couple of feet or more and by the use of dormers gain an extra room, although this technically only amounts to one-and-a-half or two-and-a-half storeys high. The side wall is developed upwards to provide a gable wall, sometimes to the height of the roof, sometimes lower, and containing a window. Internally the timbers supporting its roof interlock and are an integral part of the main roof. This creates a spacious room, albeit with slopes in places, as we have seen. In fact the Cotswold form of the dormer gable, common from the fifteenth to late seventeenth century, is almost always associated with the extended-collar type of roof construction. It is load bearing and so takes the weight of the roof truss behind it.

In the eighteenth and nineteenth centuries a much smaller type of dormer window, or more correctly a variety of types, appeared. Some of these in the Stroud valleys, often from around 1800–20, are clearly of the same date as the building itself and are integral with the purlins and wall plate of the roof. An entire section of roof is lifted, almost as in a 'letter box' shape, to lighten not a bedroom but a working area devoted to some stage of cloth manufacture. Far more common, however, were the dormers that were inserted into earlier roofs; these were not integral and could be positioned almost anywhere. They were intended to help create a new bedroom for a growing family or for servants. These dormers took on a variety of shapes, some being due to the fashion of the day or experiences of the builder. He was not at liberty, however, to put a dormer anywhere he wished, as the construction had to relate to the rafting within the roof space as we have noted above. If the window is set in a triangle of walling rising from the wall of the house and the ridge comes level with the ridge of the house, this is likely to imply an extended collar-type roof with a spacious attic as described previously. If it only extends part way the attic space will be far smaller and the bedroom ceilings may even extend up into the roof space.

Common early thatched
roof, fifteenth – eighteenth
century

Sixteenth – eighteenth century

Seventeenth century

c. 1800–1820, copied from the
mills (see page 148)

Seventeenth- and eighteenth-century variations: increasing use of
attic bedrooms

Above: Schematic illustrating variations in dormer windows.

Dormer Windows

These too are some of the most distinctive features of Cotswold houses and cottages. Initially, most roofs were thatched, as we have already observed, and the simplest way to achieve side windows on the upper floor, especially in low-walled buildings, was to raise the wall height to accommodate the window. In thatched cottages this generally produced a flowing roof form up and around the insertion, as at Chipping Campden (*bottom*).

As stone slates took over from thatch, with dormers at right angles to the main roof, the ideal form for such roofs was a simple pitch with no interruptions, and so the swept valley was introduced to turn the corner in a seamless curve before the later widespread use of lead flashing. Inverted ridge stones were often used where the ridge of the dormer was lower than the main roof, especially in the mid-Cotswolds, as we noted earlier. Illustrations here are from Willersey (*above*), and Weston Subedge, Chipping Campden (*middle, bottom* and *opposite*).

Full-Height Gables

The use of attics for weaving in the south of the region led to the building of larger dormers where a full-height gable allowed sufficient space for looms and storage. Here the ridge was at the same height as the main roof. This was often seen on grander houses, too. Examples here are from Painswick and Hidcote (*above*) and Upper Slaughter Manor (*below*) (see also Pear Tree Cottage, page 29).

Additions and Variations

The increasing use of the attic space for bedrooms led to a variety of different forms of the dormer throughout the Cotswolds, mainly in the seventeenth and eighteenth centuries. The dormer above has a roughcast-rendered gable projecting forward of the widow and supported on the extended 'ears' of the timber head.

The hipped dormer was an eighteenth-century refinement, avoiding the marked interruption of the roof slope by gables, which were then considered unfashionable; otherwise, the detailing was similar to the earlier versions.

Further Variations

The type of dormer seen on the weaver's cottages (*above*) were essentially 'copied' from those seen on nearby mills, similar to this one at Chalford (*left*).

Many other dormers have tiled gables, as shown below.

This and next page: Finials
Some early finials atop the gable end appear to have had a religious significance, as on these examples above at Wotton-under-Edge and Turkdean. Below, however, are some of the more common examples of variations on typical ball finials and other decorative features.

The Builder's Final Flourish

Adding a focal point and flourish to the gable ends, these finials, seen at Hatherop (*above*), and on Whittington Court (*below*, above the sixteenth-century, sharp-pointed gables with their Renaissance pediments) allow the mason to give expression to his skill and the owner to illustrate his standing.

Doorways

As with windows, these too illustrate the transition from a distinctive local and traditional style to the 'national' styles of the Georgian and Victorian eras.

Early cottage doorways were notable by their absence of porches providing shelter to the door itself, except for the occasional hood or slight projection of stone, and these are generally of a later date. On a number of houses, early doorways also retained the label over the top, returning down either side of the stone head or as string course.

During most of the seventeenth century the use of the lintel was almost universal and with it an almost complete absence of the arch in simpler cottages and houses. Externally the openings were never wider than the stones themselves would carry, with stout oak beams used across the door openings inside. Holly Tree Cottage, Laverton, is a typical example of the simple charm of this style with its deep head and large stones; a number can also be seen around the Stroud area. By the early eighteenth century we see some fine carved scroll brackets supporting door hoods.

The earliest surviving examples of doorways on larger houses were arched, created by having four centres from which the curve was scribed. These might be plain, or often had spandrels elaborated with leaf carvings, clothiers' trademarks or initials, especially in the Stroud valley and in Burford. The four-centred door head, made from one (locally sourced) stone, was a common treatment. Initially it was quite steep in outline but later it became flatter.

Doorways in the north-west Cotswolds particularly tended to take advantage of the fine dressed stone from the escarpment quarries with rosette and leaf carving in the spandrels and elaborate stops to the hood mould, sometimes with a date added. In Broadway and a number of surrounding villages a series of interesting doorways can be observed which appear to have been the work of one individual, or at very least certainly in a virtually identical style. Here, according to Dawber, there is a strong Gothic feeling about the shape of the door head, while the detail of the mouldings and peculiarity of the stop to the jambs all indicate evidence of the classical feeling that was finally influencing these relatively isolated districts in the north-west. Mouldings invariably finished 2 to 3 feet from the ground with chamfer stops.

Another interesting doorway can be seen in Stanton on the Warren House, which has a similar-shaped head, moulded jambs and stops and rosettes in the spandrels, but instead of the simple label there is a more classical treatment of the architrave and cornice where the builder seems to be attempting a different approach from the more traditional.

Variations in the flatter, four-centred head were achieved by inserting a keystone and/or impost stones. Rounded arches are another elaboration, generally seen on more important buildings and later finding their way on to some cottages, again reflecting an interest in the classical and absorbing Jacobean motifs – with keystones, imposts and the familiar lozenge pattern.

Throughout the southern Cotswolds (at least south of Painswick), many of the mouldings, both on doorways and windows, etc., follow the date forms used elsewhere, but are distinctly bolder and may well be a special influence asserted from Bristol workshops, although not actually prepared in Bristol.

The doorway in fact has generally been a central element, where some of the best workmanship is frequently found, often more elaborate than around windows, particularly when there is little or no ornament elsewhere to impress visitors! It was in doorways and fireplaces that the classical elements first appeared, allowing builders to express their creativity. It is especially in the external doorways and their furnishings that the Cotswold builders so excelled.

Porches, as noted, were very crude flat hoods that were added to cottages by the end of the seventeenth century. Prior to this date porches were usually an indication of an owner's status. Grander, classical porches were first introduced on high-class houses and farmhouses, built for more fashionable yeomen and clothiers.

By end of seventeenth century the use of classical features had spread down the social scale to small cottages and town houses, which made increasing use of the symmetrical front elevation. The thick stone slab hoods with shaped stone brackets that had been introduced were simple in profile or moulded as full brackets with a classical scroll form.

Though most cottages lacked a hood porch or hood of any kind, the plain doorway being left bare, this unadorned appearance has often been altered by later additions – either by an open timber variety in the Victorian period or by the use of lobbies with an outer front door, which in more recent times reflects the desire to minimise draughts and prevent heat loss.

The doors themselves were generally made of oak, with wide boards hung on long hinges, the use of a door frame only coming later (i.e. early doors closed directly into the recess cut out of the stone door surround). Not until the Georgian period were panelled doors seen in the Cotswolds in any quantity, and then usually with openings of classical proportions. Fan lights were generally plain or rectangular, and the few fan-shaped ones in the Cotswolds were generally on the grander houses.

Doors were made to proportions that became more tightly controlled as the century progressed; earlier panelled doors were tall and narrow, often with eight panels, later ones had six panels with the upper ones horizontal in emphasis (never square) and taller central panels.

Georgian and Victorian doorways became increasingly 'national' in character, gradually losing their regional flavour, though the characteristic dressed stone surrounds tended still to be used wherever this was easily acquired.

This and next page: **Doorways and Porches**

Doorways were frequently used to give expression to an owner's standing and wealth, as well as allowing builders opportunities to express their creativity. Both of these elements were used to good effect, especially on the north Cotswolds, by taking advantage of the fine dressed stone from the escarpment. The earliest surviving examples are the arched doorways; the four-centred arches, some quite plain, but often with elaborate leaf carvings in the spandrels.

Above right is the Tudor doorway now incorporated into the main building of the original Priest's House at Elkstone. In the early sixteenth-century example at Temple Guiting (*below*) the apex is somewhat more rounded by the drip moulding above. At Burford (*above left*), note the quatrefoil decoration in the spandrels.

The following page illustrates examples from the screens passage entrance to Skinner's Mill, Painswick (*top*, the fourteenth-century rear entry has a lintel replacement and the sixteenth-century front arch is due to subsequent alterations) and the early Tudor doorway at Icomb Place (*bottom*) leading to the screens end of the main hall.

Mouldings

Mouldings around the doorway also tended to become more elaborate, giving a sense of prosperity to impress the approaching visitor. The seventeenth-century examples at Western Subedge and Broadway (*above*) could very well have used the same builder, with their decorative aspects and similar chamfer stops ending some 2 feet from the ground. In the example from the Warren House at Stanton (*below right*), there is a more classical treatment of the architrave and cornice, where the builder appears somewhat less traditional in his approach.

Merchants' Marks
These are an interesting
feature of the Cotswold
region, where several
wealthy merchants had
their own marks displayed
in the spandrels above the
doorway, as, for example,
did William Selwyn at
King's Stanley in 1563
(*top*).

In Burford (*middle and
bottom*), Simon Wisdom
was a particularly wealthy
merchant who left his
initials and his mark on
several buildings in the
town.

More Marks

Wisdom's mark was remarkably similar to the one seen on Bay Tree Farm (previously Street Farm) in Nympsfield (*above*). These, and others that bear a great similarity, are open to various interpretations. Stroud also has a number of marks around the town, from Salmon Springs Mill (*bottom right*) to the gatepost entrance on The Hill (*left*, to what is now the Rotary Club and Amberley Publishing's building) and a similar one on the Rodney House in Church Street (*bottom left*).

This and next page: **Changing Arch Forms**

Rounded arches (*above*) were another form of elaboration, often on more important buildings as at the Friend's Meeting House, Nailsworth. On Daneway House (*below right*), classical influences are very apparent, still with Jacobean 'lozenge' motifs in the spandrel, clearly expressed voussoirs and prominent keystone and imposts.

Toward the end of the seventeenth century, we see the flatter pointed arch creating a simpler 'depressed' shape and a completely flat or square arch at Stanton (*next page, top right*), and a further variation of the flatter four-centred head at Broadway by the insertion of a keystone and imposts (*next page, bottom*).

Other Variations

Even more common was the plain opening with deep stone lintels, often with large dressed quoins or jamb stones forming the sides, replacing the more elaborate mouldings and stops, pictured here at Daneway House (*top left*), Sapperton and Holly Tree Cottage, Laverton (*top right*). Some also had date stones on the lintel, as at the Manor Farm in Western Subedge.

The Georgian Doorway

This essentially illustrated the end of the local vernacular, giving way to the more national style of the period. Here these elegant Georgian doorways in Chipping Campden have their classical columns, pediments and fanlights in the glazed arches over the doors. The doors themselves are always painted and are wider than modern doorways.

Above and opposite page: Porches

Quite grand classical porches were first introduced on high-class houses and farmhouses built for the more fashionable yeomen, as at Upper Swell manor (*opposite*), with its two-storey Jacobean ashlar porch and cambered pediment broken by an escutcheon of arms.

On cottages porches were rare, and these crude, flat hoods were added to many cottages by the end of the seventeenth century. Such simple hoods can be seen on the cottages above at Little Barrington.

Later Developments

By the end of seventeenth century, classical
elements had spread down the social scale to
smaller cottages and town houses. Thicker
stone hoods with strong stone brackets
were now used, with simple or more highly
decorated scrolls. Examples above are at
Little Barrington and below and right at
Chipping Campden.

Porches in Town Houses

In Marshfield, the malting industry peaked in the eighteenth century and several porches in the town reflect this trade.

In the former malthouse below, a peephole can be seen on the left-hand side of the porch, designed to keep a lookout for the exciseman! We also see a wooden lintel above the door, a much more common feature in the south Cotswolds.

Shell Hoods and Other Porches

These were added to a number of houses during the early eighteenth century, making a very attractive feature in many instances. They were generally supported on scroll brackets, as here at Barnsley, near Cirencester, and at Burford and Nailsworth.

Smaller cottages gained adornments considerably later, especially during the Victorian period, as we see in the porches and trelliswork added to the cottages in Winchcombe (*centre*). Solid lobbies with an outer front door are a more recent addition in many cottages to prevent heat loss and draughts – generally less attractive, but nevertheless functional. Cotswold cottages never had panelled doors or glass panes above the doors; these only came in as more modern additions.

This and next page: **Doors**

The doors themselves were generally made of oak and were wide-boarded and hung on hinges with a looped end dropped on to iron hooks built directly into the stonework. Door frames only came later. Some early examples are illustrated here, together with a small selection of ironwork from Berkeley Castle and Chavenage House (*next page*).

8

INTERNAL FEATURES

Chimneys and Hearths

Prior to the fifteenth century nearly all houses were heated by means of a fire on the floor, near the middle of the hall. The smoke found its way out through any number of cunning devices and evidence of smoke blackening on roof timbers can still be found in several of these older buildings.

A development of smoke bays can be seen at Bay Tree Farm, Nympsfield, where the original lintel of the hearth's smoke bay beam has been lowered to form a lintel over the large chimney corner. In its original position, not far below the ceiling, a line of moulding on its underside would have been clearly visible. But smoke bays were wasteful of both space and heat. Around 1600 they gave way to the conventional chimney corner with its internal seat, and the building of bread ovens, initially in stone, later in brick, and later still in cloam, a kind of fired clay from Barnstaple – in this case the oven came complete with its floor and dome all in one piece. Some houses had a recess for a tinderbox, candles, salt or spices where they could be kept dry. By the end of the seventeenth century the majority of parlours and many sleeping chambers had a fireplace.

Some early chimneys can still be found with their shafts pierced with an open lancet-type slit.

Apart from some forms of louvre that were purely utilitarian, there were a small number of ornate carved chimneys, but most early chimneys were simple cylindrical or octagonal ones with a moulded cap. One of these survives at The Broadwell in Dursley and others are also illustrated below.

Chimney stacks are undoubtedly among the most characteristic features of many Cotswold houses – they are substantial and solid, typical of the external treatment of fireplaces and suggesting wide inglenooks and cosy firesides. They are almost always placed centrally over the ridge or on the apex of gables at either end, and if at the side of the building then they are seen on the smaller roofs connected to the main one.

The chimney stack immediately above the roofline is generally square, with a projecting weather course above the roof slates. Once the roof is cleared the flues are often built separately, either square or diagonally, in clusters of three or four. These are made from dressed stone slabs, tied together at the top with a moulded stone cap, sometimes with an added decorative band treated as a cornice, with an architrave and frieze and often with various features as presumably took the mason's fancy.

Chimneys

A few medieval chimneys still survive, some incorporated into work of a later date. They generally take the form of octagonal or circular shafts, pierced with lancet openings and capped with a conical hood – as these at Bredon and Southrop (*above left and right*). Below right is a small octagonal one in Dursley, and one on the fifteenth-century Pigeon House at Burford (*below left*) has a restored octagonal shaft with lancet openings and original crocketed spire above.

Hearths

Prior to the fifteenth century, most houses were heated by means of a fire in the centre of the floor, the smoke finding its way out by various devices. Evidence of smoke blackening on roof timbers can be found in several older buildings, as, for example, at Skinner's Mill (*above*) – a chimney and first-floor fireplace having been inserted later.

At Nympsfield (*below*) we see evidence of an earlier smoke bay, where the original lintel has been lowered from just below the ceiling to form a lower lintel over the large chimney corner.

Chimney Stacks

The stone chimney stacks of Cotswold houses are among their most dramatic features; rising up above the roofline, often with a projecting weather course above the slates. The flues themselves are often built separately, of dressed stone, either square or diagonally and in clusters. Placed centrally over the ridge, or on the apex of a gable end, they have moulded caps, sometimes treated as a cornice, with architrave and frieze and occasionally with patterns, or even a Gothic battlemented look, as on Castle Farm at Marshfield (*opposite, top left*)– whatever took the mason's fancy.

Selected Internal Features

The general fabric was remarkably similar between cottages, smaller houses and even manor houses as regards the details of doors, windows, chimneys and roofs. The treatment of the interior, however, was greatly simplified, with little in the way of ornament or decoration as in the former. Instead of richly panelled walls and delicately fashioned plaster ceilings (as, for example, at Harrington House in Bourton-on-the-Water) we find plastered walls (though many did not have even this), roughly hewn joists of oak or elm and occasionally a moulded beam. The workmanship nevertheless remains thoroughly honest and good. In simpler buildings the work was done by local craftsmen with local materials, and frequently with a pleasing dignity and simple charm.

In the great house, after the shell was built, workmen might well be 'imported' to execute the internal finishings. It should be remembered that many of the larger houses were in the first instance built as farmhouses and later fell on hard times.

It was often on the fireplace and its surroundings that any little display of architectural design could be found.

Painswick and the Stroud valley contain many fine examples of Queen Anne and early Georgian work. Burford is another good example where some earlier circular staircases can still be found in courtyards, though they are now generally greatly 'mutilated'.

A few interesting examples of staircases are shown in the illustrations, but for greater detail and the specialist, we refer the reader to Linda Hall's informative little book which covers many of the aspects we have discussed above.

Partitions

The partitions that divide the rooms are always worthy of study, and are not always what is expected. Quite often they are of stone. But many dating from the sixteenth and seventeenth centuries are timber framed. This trait may have survived from earlier times, or even come from the notion that it might give better support to the side walls. The idea continued into the age of brick building, and even as late as the 1890s internal brick walls have a thin horizontal wooden batten inserted every few feet.

Screens also varied considerably according to the dictates of fashion. Stud and panel (sometimes called muntin and plank, cf. Brunskill, figs 220 and 229) was popular in the late sixteenth century, often made richer by the presence of a middle rail. Then came something much richer, a form of panelling with inlays and Jacobean arches. This appears in Gloucester but had a short life, no doubt because of the cost and skill involved. It gave way to the oak screens of Jacobean panelling we find in every county in the land. But look carefully at these for they deteriorate as the years go by. Instead of neat moulding around three sides there are just two or three short score lines to give the mind a false image. These screens could be used as a permanent division between two rooms, albeit a rather shaky one, or they could be fixed to a structural wall when they frequently stopped short of the ceiling, leaving a plaster strip that can be moulded or decorated with paintwork.

Fashion tired of this and by the end of the century bolection panels were all the rage. The favoured wood was now pine with the panel held forward from the face of the wall. This type of panelling was painted in gentle matt colours. Here in the Cotswolds this fashion was far less popular than in most other places and before 1700 the panels were recessed. The two styles are well seen at Dyrham Park, where rooms from 1696 and 1698–1704 adjoin each other. Distribution suggests that much of this later work was made in Bristol.

Furnishings

Two shell-hooded cupboards assumed to be by the same Bristol maker came from a house in Stroud, which is now demolished. They are dated 1714, and are displayed in Stroud's Museum in the Park. Wallpaper of this date is very rare, hand-made and often with a red or blue flock decoration. Fragments of both were found prior to demolition. On the back of one was part of a two-line name of the manufacturer, 'Blue Row Warehouse/in Aldermanbury'. This is the only known maker's name for this period ever found, and the London maker is thought to have supplied to the royal households. A much larger piece of a slightly later date is thought to date from the time of the marriage of the daughter of the original owner. This too is now in the Museum in the Park, Stroud.

Beams and Stops

At first sight one ceiling beam looks much like another. However to the expert they are very informative. They vary according to the wealth of the house builder, the relative importance of the room, the period and the region in which it is situated. The wealthy owner would seek out the best-quality wood for use in each room. But the less wealthy might use wainy timber, with the bark on in places, in the service rooms or the bedrooms. The junction of the surfaces would be chamfered but this could vary. They were quite wide, then became much narrower in the seventeenth century and by 1700 were quite rough and narrow, before the beam disappeared completely within a plastered ceiling. That said, the chamfers in the seventeenth century were much narrower in Gloucestershire than in Somerset. Here, they also changed their shape around 1600. Prior to that date they were slightly concave, after that they were convex. We are talking here about a variation of about 1 mm in a width of about 40 mm, virtually imperceptible to the naked eye or even by using a straight edge. The best way is to slap one's fingers across the chamfer and with practice the difference is very clear. There has to be a good reason for this change, the best being that a different tool had come into use.

If we look at our parish churches we find wooden screens with chamfers sometimes far more elaborate than in the houses, but nevertheless made by the same carpenters. At the end of each chamfer was an ornamental stop, a tradition going back far into medieval times. Thus in our houses we find drawn stops, scroll stops, petaloid, pyramid and drawn diamond stops, etc., made by the use of a draw-knife with minimal use of a mallet and chisel. After the mid-seventeenth century, beam stops took a multitude of complex forms, which included blocks and bars, requiring extensive use of the mallet and chisel.

Fireplaces

In the homes of the very wealthy, the fireplace was the most important and often the most ornamental feature inside the house. Where the owner had both desire and means, the head could be of stone, either plain, as at Icomb Place, or decorated, as at Chavenage (*above right*), or straight lintel, as at Blockley Manor.

In Smaller Houses and Cottages
The fireplace was a focal
point for cooking and drying
clothes after a days work, with
its heavy oak beam (often
showing the rough cuts of the
adze which formed it) and
large stone jambs. Occupants
would draw round for peace
and comfort and a sense of
belonging. On one or both sides
of the fireplace, inside the ingle,
a seat was often arranged in
the thickness of the masonry.
In the late seventeenth-century
example from Eynsham (*top*),
the original plaster in the nook
is still to be seen. Sometimes
two small niches might be
hollowed out to hold a cup or
jar. Sometimes a spice or salt
cupboard (simple or decorated)
could be found close by in the
wall to keep the contents dry.

Bread and Proving Ovens

These too were to be found at the side of the fireplace, also built into the stonework, generally with a wooden lintel, as in Elkstone (*above*), but sometimes with a more decorative stone lintel, as in the one at Painswick (*below*) with both bread and proving ovens to the left-hand side.

Modern Fireplaces

During the Victorian period, fashion again resulted in the loss of the vernacular to a large extent; nevertheless, it did result in some attractive fireplaces, as with this example at Charlbury (*above*).

However, something of a return to the vernacular can be seen at Bachelor's Court, Sapperton (*below*), in the 1913 work of Norman Jewson – complete with his initials, date and plasterwork in the surround.

Staircases

These were either a steep, simple and straight wooden flight, or of stone and circular, built into the end wall, as at Nympsfield (*above*), or to the side of a fireplace, as at Charlbury (*below*). Solid wooden treads survive, but are very rare.

Staircases

Circular staircases with a stone newel are generally only to be seen in castles, but occasionally can be found in a larger house, as at Chavenage (*top*).

Open-well staircases, favoured in larger houses, can take a number of forms. To the right is a splendid seventeenth-century example at Blockley Manor.

Other Selected Internal Features

With the advent of chimneys and the removal of often dense, smoky areas, the treatment of the interior décor of rooms changed quite dramatically in many grander houses. This is well illustrated by the 1640 coarse-weave tapestry with its forest design at Chavenage House (*top*). The detail in the middle photograph is from a substantial fragment of wallpaper salvaged from a room (redesigned around 1740, when the daughter of owner John Cole got married) in Stroud and at the bottom is a rare surviving mural in the Priest's House at Elkstone (thought to be of Ashley House and parts of Oxford). This is thought likely as the owner of Ashdown House was also Lord of Elkstone Manor at the time.

Shell Cupboards
Two shell cupboards of 1714, with
their original painted decoration,
were rescued from John Cole's house
prior to its demolition several decades
ago. They were probably made in
Bristol. (Courtesy of the Museum in
the Park, Stroud)

Panelled Walls

Subtly painted wooden panels were used to hide the rough stonework beneath in a number of fine houses, as well as acting as (rather flimsy) divisions between rooms in several cases. As noted in the main text, this and other panelling changed quite quickly according to different tastes of the time, and so lost much of its intrinsic local craftsmanship. Above are examples of late sixteenth- and early seventeenth-century work at Painswick and Sydenhams, and below is similarly dated work from Chavenage House, together with early and late seventeenth-century panelling at Salmon Springs Mill.

Plaster Ceilings

Delicately plastered ceilings would also be found in high-status houses, as this rococo work of 1740 in Harrington House, Bourton-on-the-Water, clearly illustrates (*above*). Decorative plaster ceilings, however, were not as common in Gloucestershire as in adjoining counties, and many have been lost during house modernisations. Horton Court (*below left*) has a plaster ceiling, but this is of a much more modern date, just prior to the middle of the last century (around 1937).

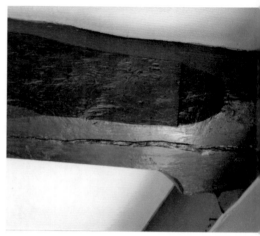

Beams and Stops

Much can be learnt from close inspection of the ends of ceiling beams, even if, superficially, one does look very much like another. Some indication of these various facets, briefly described in the text and selectively illustrated here, give an idea of the specialist knowledge required to interpret and date the various subtle differences. For instance, differences in the chamfers, between convex and concave, can really only be determined by running one's fingers across them. The reason for these subtle differences is presumably the use of different tools – use of an adze to provide a slightly hollowed chamfer before 1600, and use of a broad axe or hook to give a slightly convex chamfer after 1600.

Pyramidal and scroll stops are seen on these sixteenth-century beams at Skinner's Mill, Painswick (*above*), and a broad chamfer with a scroll stop is pictured at Salmon Springs (*below*).

Also at Salmon Springs is an unusual, possibly seventeenth-century, stop and an early seventeenth-century stop with fleur-de-lis decoration on the chamfer.

Final Thoughts

As the Victorian writers would have said, 'As we lay down our pen...' This story of Cotswold houses is almost as large and complicated as it can get without becoming too technical and impersonal. It should be clear by now that the Cotswold scene is a very varied one, with many elements that are often counter to one's internalised images. Nevertheless, as we have endeavoured to show, there are many aspects that give these elements a distinctive and recognisable flavour. We have covered long distances and watched man's contribution over the centuries. The rich and the poor 'made' the area, each in their different ways. One unique factor is the local pride of the region that meant craftsmen maintained the individual style, when in almost every other area it was stifled by fashion and artificial values. Here the style continues, not as some pastiche but as an emotive issue from the heart.

We hope that this work may lead you, through better understanding, to find even greater enjoyment in your environment. The story is not complete; there are countless new things waiting to be found and to be interpreted, but sketching details and drawing precise plans all take time. There is ample scope for another lifetime of research. Alas, that is beyond our control. We hope others will take on the challenge as we leave off.

The Cotswold style lives on.

BIBLIOGRAPHY

General Works

Barley, M. W., *The English Farmhouse and Cottage*, London: Routledge & Kegan Paul 1961

Brunskill, R. W., *Timber Building in Britain*, London: Yale University Press 1994

Cook, O. & E. Smith, *English Cottages and Farmhouses*, B.C.A. 1982

Cordigley, R. A., 'British Historical Roof-Types and their Members', *Trans. Ancient Monuments Soc.* 1961

Davis, P. R., *Hearth & Home: The Story of the Welsh House*, Hereford: Logaston 2009

Ditchfield, P. H. & S. R. Jones, *The Manor Houses of England*, Batsford: London 1910

Hall, L., *Period House Fixtures and Fittings 1300–1900*, Newbury: Countryside Books 2005

Morris, R. K., *The Archaeology of Buildings*, Stroud: Tempus 2004

Platt, C., *Medieval England*, B.C.A. 1978

Quiney, A., *The Traditional Buildings of England*, London: Thames & Hudson 1990

Weaver, Sir L., *Cottages: Their Planning, Design and Materials*, London: Country Life 1926

Wood, M., *The English Medieval House*, London: Ferndale Editions 1981

Regional Studies

Alcock, N. & D. Miles, *The Medieval Peasant House in Midland England*, Oxford: Oxbow 2013

Bright, G. V., 'Picturesque Gloucestershire', Cheltenham: Cheltenham Newspaper Co. Ltd. 1928

Brill, E., *Life and Tradition on the Cotswolds*, London: J. M. Dent 1973

Catchpole, A., D. Clark & R. Peberdy, *Burford: Buildings and People in a Cotswold Town*, Chichester: Phillimore 2008

Cooke, R., *West Country Houses*, Bristol: private publication 1957

Davie, W. G. & E. G. Dawber, *Old Cottages, Farm-houses & and Other Stone Buildings in the Cotswold District*, London: Batsford 1905

Fox, C. & Raglan, *Monmouthshire Houses 1415–1714*, 3 vols, Cardiff: National Museum of Wales 1951–54

Gordan, C., *Cotswold Arts and Crafts Architecture*, Chichester: Phillimore 2009

Hall, L. J., *The Rural Houses of North Avon & South Gloucestershire 1400–1720*, Bristol: Bristol Museum & Art Gallery 1983

Hill, M. & S. Birch, *Cotswold Stone Homes*, Thrupp: Sutton Publishing 1994

Jordan, T., *Cotswold Barns*, Stroud: Tempus 2006, reprinted in 2010 by The History Press

Jordan, T., *Cotswold Stone Barns*, Stroud: Amberley 2011

Kingsley, N., *The Country Houses of Gloucestershire 1500–1660*, Cheltenham 1989

Kingsley, N., *The Country Houses of Gloucestershire 1660–1830*, Chichester: Phillimore 1992

Kingsley, N. & M. Hill, *The Country Houses of Gloucestershire 1830–2000*, Chichester: Phillimore 2001

Mander, N., *Country Houses of the Cotswolds*, London: Aurum 2008

Paterson, N. M., *The Vernacular Architecture & Buildings of Stroud & Chalford*, Oxford: Trafford 2006

Slocombe, P. M., *Wiltshire Farmhouses & Cottages, 1500–1580*, Devizes 1988

Slocombe, P. M., *Wiltshire Farm Buildings, 1500–1900*, Devizes 1989

Slocombe, P. M., *Medieval Houses of Wiltshire*, Stroud: Sutton 1992

Slocombe, P. M., *Wiltshire Town Houses 1500–1900*, Trowbridge 2001

Verey, D. & A. Brooks, *The Buildings of England, Gloucestershire 1. Cotswolds*, London: Penguin 1999

Verey, D. & A. Brooks, *The Buildings of England, Gloucestershire 2. The Vale & the Forest of Dean*, London: Yale 2002

Walrond, L. F. J. and C. Powell, 'The Medieval Houses of Rural Gloucestershire', in A. Saville (ed.), *Archaeology in Gloucestershire*, Cheltenham 1984

Walrond, L. F. J., 'Medieval Smoke Vents & Low Room Walls in the Severn Plain', in *Trans. Bristol & Glos. Archaeological Soc.* Vol. 103, 1987

Wood-Jones, R. B., *Traditional Domestic Architecture of the Banbury Region*, Manchester: Manchester University Press 1963

ACKNOWLEDGEMENTS

The authors would like to express their deep gratitude to the owners and occupiers of the many houses visited over several years, and to all who have given help and advice in many ways. Particular thanks go to Arthur Price, members of the Vernacular Architecture group and to the Gloucestershire and Oxfordshire Buildings Recording Groups. To Peter Keene of Thematic Trails for his patience in producing yet another version of the map, John Richards of JR Media for his technical wizardry with old negatives and to the Museum in the Park, Stroud, for permission to use photographs of the shell cupboards and wallpaper in their collection. Finally to the staff at Amberley Publishing, without whose enthusiasm, support and patience our affection for this region and delight in its buildings would never have come to fruition.

INDEX

Also available from Amberley Publishing

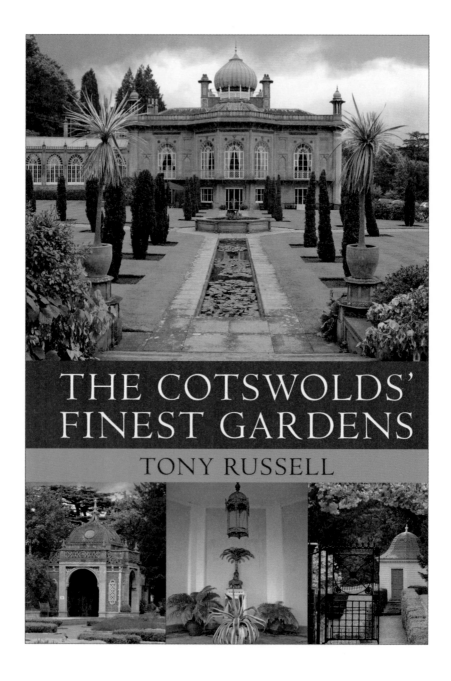

THE COTSWOLDS'
FINEST GARDENS

TONY RUSSELL

Available from all good bookshops or to order direct
Please call **01453-847-800**
www.amberleybooks.com